MW00743884

Love, Joy, and Peace

The Fruit of the Spirit

Lane Burgland

Contributions by Edward Engelbrecht

CONCORDIA PUBLISHING HOUSE • SAINT LOUIS

Contents

About This Series

This is to My Father's glory, that you bear much fruit, showing your-selves to be My disciples.

Jesus, *John 15:8*

Only hours before Jesus was arrested, He delivered an important message to His disciples (John 14–16). At the heart of this message He describes the "fruit" His disciples would bear, the works they would do to glorify the heavenly Father. Through the gift of the Spirit, Jesus promised love (John 14:21), joy (15:11), and peace (14:27) to them and to you.

However, many Christian families and congregations lack the love, joy, and peace Jesus described. Selfishness, pride, and abusive behavior arise all to easily for us. Sin is truly second nature to human beings, even to the people of God.

This Bible study series will help you produce the fruit God calls you to bear as a believer. Through biblical examples and teaching from both the Old and New Testaments, you will explore God's goodness and blessings for you in Christ. You will learn to crucify "the sinful nature with its passions and desires" and "live by the Spirit" (Galatians 5:24, 25).

Student Introduction

Good living begins with good understanding. For this reason Jesus spent considerable time teaching His disciples before sending them out in service. Among the things Jesus taught His disciples was "Every good tree bears good fruit" (Matthew 7:17). In other words, God's people will naturally want to do His will by doing good works.

Unfortunately, Jesus' illustration about good trees bearing good fruit has been used as a reason to ignore Christian education about good works. The argument has been made that, since Christians will naturally bear fruit and do good works, there's no point preaching or teaching about them. There's no point in studying them. Just let nature take its course.

Certainly you and all God's people need to have confidence that God's Word and teaching will lead to good works. But no congregation can ignore the truth that the sinful nature is still very much at work within the people of God (Romans 7:15–19). You need constant pruning! Jesus also taught, "Remain in Me, and I will remain in you. No branch can bear fruit by itself; it must remain in the vine. Neither can you bear fruit unless you remain in Me" (John 15:4). He called you to cling to both the Law of His teaching (which commands good works) and the Gospel (which causes good works to grow).

The Work of the Spirit

When the apostle Paul wrote to the Christians in Galatia about the "fruit of the Spirit," he wrote to a congregation afflicted with sin. The Galatians had eagerly embraced the Gospel. But soon after the apostle left to preach elsewhere, the Galatians divided into factions and were carried away by false doctrine. They erred in the most basic ways by confusing God's Law and Gospel (3:2–3), attacking one another (5:15), and growing conceited (5:26; 6:3). They had lost the love, joy, and peace first cultivated by the apostle's preaching. In response, Paul writes to them not only about correct doctrine (ch. 1–4) but also about Christian behavior: the fruit of the Spirit (ch. 5–6).

The list of the "fruit of the Spirit" in Galatians 5 is not the only list of good works recorded in the apostle Paul's letters. (See 2 Corinthians 6:6; Ephesians 4:2; Colossians 3:12; 1 Timothy 6:11; and 2 Timothy 2:22 for other examples.) Yet it is Paul's most complete list and is especially directed to congregational members rather than church leaders. In this list of nine "fruit," the apostle summarizes what Christ wants to cultivate in you by His Spirit.

You did not choose Me, but I chose you and appointed you to go and bear fruit—fruit that will last. Then the Father will give you whatever you ask in My name. This is My command: Love each other.
(John 15:16–17)

To prepare for "The Way of Love," read Genesis 27.

1

The Way of Love

How do I love thee? Let me count the ways.

Elizabeth Barrett Browning, *Sonnets from the Portuguese, #43*

In the 13 lines that follow this famous question from Elizabeth Barrett Browning, the poetess provides her answer: "I love thee to the depth and breadth and height my soul can reach." She concludes in the last line: "and, if God choose, I shall but love thee better after death."

Browning's poem uses the word *love* in a most noble way. Yet the word *love* can mean so much less. We use it to describe our feelings about all kinds of things and people: "I love my dog," "I love pizza," "I love my children," "I love sunny days," and so on. "Love" ranges from mere preference to the greatest emotion humans are capable of experiencing. We can even say that we "love to hate" someone or something!

If we focus on love within human relationships, we can discuss sexual love, family love, friendship, and more. This study will explore what the word *love* means when it is used in the Old and New Testaments. It will conclude by exploring what the Bible teaches about the love God gives us through His Son, Jesus Christ.

1. Before looking up a single Bible passage, take a moment to write a brief definition of the word *love*. At the end of this chapter you will compare what you have learned with what you have written below.

Family Love

The Old Testament abounds with stories of families. Like modern families, these people experienced conflict, hardship, and trouble, all in the context of the natural love that members of a family have for one another. When we read these stories, we find that "love" often plays a part in family strife.

When God created Adam and Eve, He gave them the first command: "Be fruitful and increase in number; fill the earth and subdue it" (Genesis 1:28). He established marriage as the context in which they were to fulfill His command (Genesis 2:22–24). Two types of love come together at this point: erotic love (between Adam and Eve) and family love (as their family grows). However, sin destroys love of all types. After the fall into sin, Adam blamed Eve rather than protecting her (Genesis 3:12); he followed her into sin rather than leading her in obedience to God's command (Genesis 3:6).

In the story of Cain and Abel (Genesis 4) we see the hideous fruit sin can produce in a family. What God created for love and security became a cauldron of hate and violence when sin took control. Love, as God created it, looks to the welfare of another person. Sin, as man embraced it, looks selfishly only towards personal welfare. Instead of "God first, you second, me third," sin produces the heartfelt conviction of "me first, me only, and me always."

Read below two "case studies" of family love. The first reveals a great deal of conflict where we would expect family love. The second shows family love where we might not expect it.

Isaac and Rebekah

We begin with Isaac and Rebekah, blessed with twin boys who began sibling rivalry early. Genesis 25:19–26 describes their birth and the midwife's effort to identify the firstborn.

2. Why was it so important to determine which son was born first? See Deuteronomy 21:15–17 for help.

3. How might the rights of the firstborn affect the relationship between family members?

4. Briefly discuss issues of fairness in family matters. How is love different from favoritism?

The same word used by Moses to describe the birthright of the firstborn in Deuteronomy 21:17 (*habekorah*) also appears in Genesis 25:34 as the gifts Esau despised. In Genesis 43:33 Joseph seats each of his brothers "according to his birthright" (the phrase "according to his birthright" occurs in the original Hebrew but is altered by some translations).

The status of firstborn for a descendant in Abraham's family would have conferred on Esau both a birthright (to inherit a double portion of his family's wealth) as well as a blessing (to be the ancestor of the coming Savior, a promise made to Abraham in Genesis 12:1–3). Although God permitted such cultural conventions, Genesis shows that He also overturns them. He chose Jacob as the son through whom the line of promise would continue, even though Jacob was the younger son. Later, God chose Judah (the fourth-born son of Jacob) to be the bearer of the promised line rather than any of his three older brothers: Reuben, Simeon, and Levi. We will never know how God might have brought this about without Jacob's scheming. One amazing fact stands out despite all the deception and favoritism: God works His saving will even through the sinful acts of His people!

5. Read Genesis 25:27–34. Esau sells his birthright to Jacob. What does this passage reveal about the family love between these two brothers?

Genesis 27 describes a remarkable web of relationships within Isaac's family, as illustrated on page 10. The arrows in the diagram represent the complexity of interaction between family members. Explore the complexity of family life and family love by considering each relationship in Genesis 27.

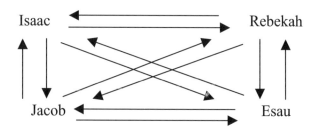

6. Read Genesis 27:1–4. Summarize the relationship between Isaac and Esau.

7. Read Genesis 27:5–17. Summarize the relationship between Rebekah and Isaac.

8. How do these events reflect on the relationship between Isaac and Rebekah?

9. Read Genesis 27:18–29. What do Isaac's actions tell you about the state of the family?

10. Read Genesis 27:30–41. How do these events change the relationship between Jacob and Esau?

Many years after the events of Genesis 25–27, God called the prophet Malachi to reassure the people of Israel that He loved them. They had been through the Babylonian exile and had rebuilt the temple in Jerusalem, yet they were discouraged and in danger of losing hope. Their nation was poor and small, they didn't seem to have much of a future, and they began to doubt God's promises. Malachi begins his book by reminding them of their roots.

11. Read Malachi 1:2–3. How does this passage describe God's love?

12. Do "love" and "hate" mean something more than simple emotions in this passage? Can "love" be a decision, an act of the will, as well as a feeling or an emotion?

Malachi's teaching about God's "hate" shocks and offends the sensibilities of many people. They wonder, "How can a loving heavenly Father speak this way?" But think about it. If God loves what is good, how would He respond to what is evil and destroys His dear creation (Psalm 5:4–5)? How do you respond to the evils that threaten the good of your family or community? Love compels God and His people to choose between good and evil.

Thanks be to God, He did not reject His fallen, broken creation but lovingly planned for its salvation. Through sinners like Jacob and the people of Israel, He brought forth the truest expression of His love: the sinless life and personal sacrifice of His Son, Jesus, for the sins of the whole world. This is the depth of love God has for you! Though your sin offends His holiness and righteousness, His fatherly love constrains His heart. In Holy Baptism He washes away your sins. He lovingly embraces you as His dear child through Christ. Though you lie and deceive like Jacob and Rebekah, though you despise His blessings like Esau, He extends His gracious hand in mercy as if to say, "Come here, My child, and kiss Me" (cf. Genesis 27:26). He makes you the heir of all the blessings that belong to His firstborn, Jesus.

See in Jacob's story and in Malachi's words the passionate heart of God's love for you fulfilled in Christ Jesus.

Boaz and Ruth

The Book of Ruth contains another "case study" of family love. Although the word *love* appears only once in the entire book in most translations (Ruth 4:15), we can see love woven throughout the story. In contrast to the dysfunctional family dynamics of Isaac and Rebekah, Naomi's relationship with her daughter-in-law Ruth reveals a depth of affection and degree of sacrifice seldom seen between blood relatives, much less between in-laws.

The author of Ruth sketches the events that lead up to Naomi's return to Israel. Tragedy and loss marked her life when her husband and two sons died in Moab, a pagan nation next to Israel. When Naomi returned, both daughters-in-law tried to stay with her but she discouraged them. They had no future with her and only a difficult, lonely life awaited them in Israel.

13. How does Ruth measure her love for Naomi in 1:16–17?

14. Jump ahead to Ruth 2:1–12. What attracts Boaz to Ruth? Are there other reasons he shows these kindnesses to Ruth?

15. Read Ruth 4:2–8. What price does Boaz, Naomi's kinsman-redeemer, pay for his love of Ruth?

The figure of the kinsman-redeemer is hidden by some translations that use "close relative" or "next of kin" to translate *hagoel* in Ruth 4:1, 6, and 8. The idea behind "redeem" is the payment of a purchase price to reacquire a person. A good example of this is in Hosea 3:2, where Hosea buys his wife back for a combination of cash and goods (the word *redeem* does not appear there).

16. The love and care that Boaz and Ruth shared had consequences far beyond their own relationship. Their love affects your life today! Read Ruth 4:17–22 and Matthew 1:5. To what blessings did their love lead? How has this affected you and your family?

Erotic Love

In English we sometimes use the word *love* to refer to sexual activity, without any higher emotion or commitment involved. "To make love" can mean little more than following the natural impulse to have intercourse. Biblical writers sometimes use *love* in the same way. Ezekiel frequently condemned God's people for their idolatry using a comparison with adultery. God (the husband) condemned Israel (the wife) for her involvement with other gods (her lovers), whom she chased with a passion (lust). We see this use of *love* in Ezekiel 16:33, 36, 37; 23:5, 9, and 22 (see also Hosea 2:7; 3:1; Jeremiah 22:20, 22; and 30:14—NIV translates "lovers" as "allies"). Because of Ezekiel's blunt and powerful imagery, Jewish Bible students were not allowed to read his book until they passed their 30th birthday!

Nevertheless, sexuality is a very important part of God's design for us. It is the means to "be fruitful and increase in number [multiply]" (Genesis 1:28). It is the "one flesh" union mentioned in Genesis 2:24 (1 Corinthians 6:16 uses this passage in reference to illicit sexual union with prostitutes, showing us that "one flesh" means sexual intercourse).

17. How important is erotic love in God's plan for humankind? How important is erotic love for marriage? for modern society?

In the real world, the various types of love often come together in a single relationship. Between husband and wife, especially over a period of time, all varieties of love appear: sexual attraction, family bonding, deep friendship, and sacrificial self-giving. Yet even where all these "loves" live together, one type may dominate at any given time.

The relationship between husband and wife is rich, complex, challenging, and fruitful—not to mention confusing, humorous, and (at times) painful. We see this in the Song of Solomon (also called Song of Songs), a biblical poem that celebrates love, as bride and bridegroom rejoice in their new relationship, bonded by love in all its rich complexity.

The Song opens with the bride inviting her bridegroom to come to her and enjoy the physical, erotic aspect of their union (1:2, 4). The most common title the bride uses of the bridegroom is "beloved" (almost two dozen times, derived from the same root word as the name David). The bridegroom calls out to her in 1:9, addressing her as "my darling."

18. What does the bridegroom call his bride in Song of Solomon 2:2, 10, 13; 4:1, 7; 5:2; 6:4?

19. How does the bridegroom address the bride in 4:9, 10, 12; 5:1, 2?

20. What types of love are suggested by the Song's terms ("neighbor," "sister," and "bride")?

21. How does the author describe this complex combination of love in its various forms (see especially 8:6–7)?

22. *For personal reflection. Sharing optional.* If you are married, consider which expression of love from the Song of Solomon describes your love for your spouse. Why does this describe your spouse?

23. Close your eyes while one member of the class slowly reads aloud Isaiah 54:4–8. Consider and discuss the passions the Lord describes. List the kind words the "husband" speaks to His wife.

24. How does this passage help you understand the depth of God's love for you in Christ?

Friendship

We turn now to a third type of love, different from family love and from erotic love. In family love, the bond of blood or commitment unites people in a lasting relationship. With erotic love, passion unites with commitment to form a bond that God designed to last a lifetime. Friendship, on the other hand, can be more difficult to nail down. For example, we might form a close bond of friendship while we are away at school or in military service. Perhaps we think that we will always stay in touch with others when our education or military obligation ends. Most often we do not stay in touch. Years pass without anything more than a Christmas card (if that). Yet if we come together again those years melt away and it is as if we were transported back to the days when the friendship was a vital and living part of our daily lives.

In the Old Testament, one friendship stands above all the others—the friendship of David and Jonathan.

25. Most people know who David was, but who was Jonathan? Read 1 Samuel 13:2, 16.

God directed Samuel to anoint David as the future king of Israel (1 Samuel 16:1–13), so that he would eventually replace the current king, Saul. Since Saul was Jonathan's father, David and Jonathan should have been bitter enemies. But they formed a deep and abiding friendship. David, not Jonathan, would sit on Saul's throne after the king died. In spite of that, Jonathan loved David as much as his own life (1 Samuel 18:1). Read 1 Samuel 18 and 20 to find out more about the friendship between David and Jonathan.

26. What is a "covenant" and what does it say about the friendship between David and Jonathan in 18:3–4? about friendship in general?

27. What covenant does Jonathan establish with David in 20:12–17?

Many friendships develop around particular activities. We cultivate friendships with people who enjoy what we enjoy. Real friendship goes beyond this or any single activity. The pleasure of each other's company, even when there is no conversation or activity, becomes important. Consider what experiences forge a friendship and how a friendship is maintained over a long time. By way of comparison and contrast, discuss the friendship between God and Abraham or God and Moses (Exodus 33:11; Isaiah 41:8; 2 Chronicles 20:7).

28. Contrast the growing relationship between David and Jonathan with the relationship David had with Saul, Jonathan's father. (See especially 1 Samuel 18:28–29 and 20:30–31.) Are there times when a loving friendship is more important than a family relationship? Explain your answer.

29. Read 1 Samuel 31:1–2, 8 and 2 Samuel 21:13–14 to find out how David and Jonathan's friendship ended. Reflect on how Jonathan balanced his loyalty towards his father with his friendship with David.

How do you handle a situation where two loves, such as family love and friendship, conflict with each other?

Love for God

"Love the LORD your God with all your heart and with all your soul and with all your strength" (Deuteronomy 6:4). "Love your neighbor as yourself" (Leviticus 19:18). On these two commands hangs the whole Law. (See Mark 12:30–31 and Matthew 22:37, 39.) After investigating "love" in family, between spouses, and among friends, we now look at a different but related type of love—mankind's love for God.

In a way, each of the previous three types of love find a parallel here: God is our Father (family love), and we are united in faith with Him (reminding us of the union of husband and wife). Because we are His people, we are also His friends, as were Moses (Exodus 33:11) and Abraham (Isaiah 41:8; 2 Chronicles 20:7); "friend" in both passages translates a form of "my loved one."

At this point in our study, we want to ask what God means when He commands us to love Him with all our heart, soul, mind, and strength and to love our neighbors as ourselves.

30. Identify several distinctive elements of love for God from the following Bible verses:

Genesis 3:1–7

Deuteronomy 6:1–3

Jeremiah 2:2

Genesis 22:1–12

Ever since mankind's "leap" into sin, each person comes into the world as a self-centered and selfish being. This destroys our relationship with God and twists every other social connection throughout our lives. We have seen how this affected some of the people and the families in the Old Testament.

We find that the love God calls us to have for Him and our neighbor is far more than mere emotion, greater than social bonding, and stronger than fleeting infatuation. It involves an act of the will, a commitment of the heart, and all the strength of our lives.

God commands us to put Him first in our lives and to consider the welfare of others just as important to us as our own welfare is. God is not talking about a "psychological self-acceptance" or "emotional self-affirmation" when He commands us to love our neighbors as ourselves. What He has in mind is a value system where other people are just as valuable as we are to ourselves.

It is, to put it bluntly, impossible to live up to this standard of love. We cannot do it. Human love looks and behaves much more like the dysfunctional family of Isaac than the ideal love God demands in the Law.

31. In Galatians 5:22, Paul put love first in his list of "the fruit of the Spirit." What might we conclude from its place in the list? Read Galatians 5:6b, 14.

How mysteriously God reveals His love! Because He loved Israel He gave them His covenant, a covenant that they could not keep. Yet this, too, was an act of love and mercy. The covenant showed the Israelites how incomplete their love was. In this way, the Lord taught them to cry out to Him, to seek from Him something more than commandments (Deuteronomy 4:30–31). He taught them to cry out for His compassion, His love.

After Moses gave the people the Ten Commandments he told them, "The LORD did not set His affection on you and choose you because you were more numerous than other peoples, for you were the fewest of all peoples. But it was because the LORD loved you and kept the oath He swore to your forefathers that He brought you out with a mighty hand and redeemed you from the land of slavery, from the power of Pharaoh king of Egypt. Know therefore that the LORD your God is God; He is the faithful God, keeping His covenant of love to a thousand generations of those who love Him and keep His commands" (Deuteronomy 7:7–9). This abiding, redeeming love of God for Israel pointed forward to the new covenant that He would provide through the perfect life, death, and resurrection of Jesus.

18

32. Look back at your answer to question 1 (p. 7) about the meaning of the word *love*. How have the examples and teachings of Scripture helped you grow in your understanding of love?

Words to Remember

Love the LORD your God with all your heart and with all your soul and with all your strength. Deuteronomy 6:5

To prepare for "God Is Love," read 1 John

2

God Is Love

Once for all, then, a short precept is given to you: Love and do what you will. . . . Let the root of love be within—from this root can nothing spring except what is good.

Augustine, *The First Epistle of St. John, Homily VII.8*

Christians begin their lives as part of a family, develop friends as they grow up, and most often fall in love and get married. Family love, friendship, and erotic love all form part of the Christian experience in life, just as they do for non-Christians. So what is different about the love Christians share? Nothing . . . and everything.

As human beings, we Christians live our lives as other people do. We do not renounce our parents, abandon our children, avoid social contacts, and give up marriage on account of Christ. God did not design us to live as hermits (Genesis 2:18). Faith in Jesus Christ does not invalidate our relationships. Rather, the Holy Spirit reshapes our mind through this faith (Titus 3:4–5). Our attitude and way of thinking about the world changes radically as a result of the new relationship we have with God through Jesus Christ (Romans 12:1–2; Philippians 3:4–7).

God creates a whole new person each time an individual receives the Sacrament of Baptism, as Paul confirms in 2 Corinthians 5:17; Galatians 6:15; Ephesians 2:10 and 4:24. Yet the old human nature remains, centered on itself and seeking its own welfare. Christians fight a battle throughout life, experiencing an internal conflict between the new person (created by the Holy Spirit) and the old nature (inherited from Adam). Two opposing value systems, two completely different ways of looking at the world, two mutually incompatible attitudes exist in us Christians every moment of our lives on earth. Because of this, Christians often do not show the love that characterizes God's family. The old nature, our "default setting," sets the agenda for our lives too often and controls our daily conduct. Each day the Christian faces the challenge of overcoming this self-centered and self-seeking way of thinking and living. This is possible only through the work of God in our hearts, minds, and souls.

33. Reflect on the internal struggle faced by believers. Can you think of specific examples of such struggle?

Family Love

The earthly family, which is the building block for all society, reflects the heavenly family. Family unity is a physical reflection of the unity of the three persons in the Godhead. According to the apostle Paul, the husband is head over his wife in God's design, as the Father is head of the Son within the Trinity (1 Corinthians 11:3). The wife submits herself to her husband, as the Son submits to the Father within the Godhead. In 1 Corinthians 11:3, Jesus submits Himself to the Father eternally, not just in His state of humiliation, as revealed in 15:27–28.

The institution of "family," imaging humanity's Creator, provides a wonderful working model for our investigation of Christian family love. The first epistle of John, a letter written to a family of faith traumatized by division and doubt, helps us discover true, spiritual "family values."

34. How do we have a family bond with the Father and the Son? Read 1 John 1:1–4 and John 3:5–6.

35. What are the "family characteristics" of God's children (1 John 1:5–7; 2:3–6)? Contrast this with the distinctive features of Satan's "family" in 1 John 2:9–11. (See also John 8:31–47.)

36. If God loves the world (John 3:16), why shouldn't we love it also (1 John 2:15–17)?

37. How is Christian love for fellow believers connected to "doing righteousness" (1 John 3:10)? How do we know what John means by "righteousness" (1 John 2:29; 3:7)?

38. What kind of love is John talking about in 1 John 4:7?

39. How can love be an obligation, as described in 1 John 4:11? See also John 13:35; 15:17.

40. In the family of God, how is love for God connected with love for other believers (1 John 4:13–5:1)?

Erotic Love

Husband and wife share a natural affection for each other. We can see this from Adam's exclamation in Genesis 2:23. He had reviewed and named all the animals under his supervision but had found no suitable "helper" (Genesis 2:19–20). The dramatic movement of the story, beginning in 2:18 with the first pronouncement of "good" in creation, now reaches its crescendo in 2:23, "This is now bone of my bones and flesh of my flesh; she shall be called 'woman,' for she was taken out of man." His joy at seeing Eve for the first time reflects the love and compatibility that God intended for husband and wife. Does faith in Christ Jesus change this? In other words, does the love between a Christian husband and wife differ from that of non-Christians?

We can answer both no and yes. Christians, like everyone else, have the natural emotions of our species and go through the same experiences as other human beings. So how does the love of God in Christ Jesus reshape and reform the natural love between husband and wife in the family of God? We turn to Ephesians 5:21–33 for the answer. (Note that 5:21 forms a "hinge verse" connecting the preceding paragraphs with this section.)

In these verses Paul discusses three sets of relationships—wife and husband, child and parent, employee (slave) and employer (slave owner). He addresses the *subordinate* individual first and then turns his attention to the leaders in the relationships (i.e., the *superordinate*). While we want to focus on the husband-and-wife relationship, we also want to note parallels with the other relationships.

41. What common directions does Paul give to wives (5:22), children (6:1), and employees (6:5)?

42. What elements are common to the callings (vocations) of husbands in 5:25, fathers in 6:4, and employers in 6:9?

43. Many people today struggle to understand Ephesians 5:22, which is commonly read at church weddings. What does the modern ear hate to hear in Paul's commands to wives (5:22)? Why? (See Genesis 3:1–7.)

44. What does Paul say to husbands (5:25–27) that he does not say to fathers and employers?

45. How is marriage a "mystery"?

Paul instructs a wife to "fear" her husband (Ephesians 5:33 ASV). Some translations offer "respect" (like the NIV, ESV, NKJV, NRSV) or "reverence" (KJV). The key to understanding "fear" in this passage is the biblical phrase "fear of the LORD." This "fear" includes respect and reverence, but its central feature is saving faith (as is obvious in 2 Chronicles 19:9; Proverbs 14:27; 19:23; Isaiah 11:2–3; 33:6; Acts 10:34–35). Thus Paul advises wives to trust their husbands, submitting to their husbands as the church submits to the Lord. Paul does not mean that a wife must cower in the presence of her husband.

46. Read 1 John 4:18. What effect does love have upon fear?

Friendship

Friendship is a choice. We are born into a family, we fall into love, we go to school with our neighbors, and we work with our colleagues. However, we choose our friends. Jesus sums up a common natural approach to friendship in Matthew 5:43—we love our friends and hate our enemies.

The fruit of the Spirit differs markedly from this attitude because the Christian reflects God's own mind in this matter. We should remember that Christ Jesus died for us while we were enemies of God (see Romans 5:8, 10). Because of the cross, Christian friendship differs greatly from other friendship. Take, for example, the story of the Good Samaritan (Luke 10:25–37).

47. Read 2 Kings 17:24 and John 4:9. What was the relationship between the Samaritans and the Jews?

48. What question prompted Jesus to tell the story of the Good Samaritan (Luke 10:25–29)?

49. What point does Jesus make through this parable? How does this answer the question (v. 25) from the expert in the Law?

50. How can we be a friend to every human being we encounter in our life?

We turn next to a working definition of friendship. What Paul says about love in 1 Corinthians 13 reflects a choice much more than an emotion. It is a choice based on what we have received, not on the qualities or character of the person we want to be our friend. Even though we often hear this text at weddings, Paul is not writing about erotic love or even family love. In this passage, he describes the friendship that Christians offer not only to other members of God's family but also to everyone we encounter.

51. List the qualities of Christian love (13:4–8). How closely do we resemble this description in our relationships, particularly with people we don't like?

52. By faith we receive God's blessings. In hope we await the resurrection and eternal life. Why does the apostle call Christian love greater than faith and hope?

53. How may we bridge the gap between our lives and Paul's description of love in this passage? Read 1 John 4:7–12.

Christ the Ideal

The sinner who encounters God outside of Jesus Christ finds only judgment and righteous condemnation. Only through Jesus Christ, by means of saving faith in Him who died and rose for us, do we find that "God is love." Along with such confessions of faith as "God is Spirit" (John 4:24) and "God is light" (1 John 1:5), John tells us that "God is love" (1 John 4:8, 16). The way John writes these confessions of faith affirms that "God" is bigger than one simple attribute or characteristic.

Moved by love for the hostile, alienated world, God sent His only-begotten Son to pay the Law's penalty against lawbreakers. (The original verb tense of *loved* in John 3:16 strongly suggests the singular event of the cross rather than a general comment about God's love.) God does not love the world because it possesses some lovable quality or noble virtue. God's love in Christ Jesus originates within God Himself, independent of our good deeds, physical appearance, ethnic origin, individual character, or social standing. Jesus shows us the nature of perfect love as He lays down His life for His enemies, sacrificing Himself for a world that would not recognize or accept Him. The sacrifice of the cross becomes the working model for Christian love.

54. Read 1 John 3:11–15. Compare the way of Cain with the way of Christ. Both ways culminate in a death. Both involve passion. Yet how are they different?

Perhaps the most popular "love" story in Western culture is the story of Romeo and Juliet. In this story, the groom kills himself because he believes that his bride has died. The bride then kills herself because she finds that her husband has died. They commit suicide because they fear that they will not be together.

55. Like the story of Cain and the story of Jesus, the story of Romeo and Juliet also involves passion and death. Is this popular story of love one that Christians should imitate? Why or why not?

56. John says we should imitate Christ by laying down our lives for fellow Christians (1 John 3:16). No one reading this study has died for the sake of fellow Christians (or else you wouldn't be reading this!). Are you failing to live by the love Christ calls you to? Why or why not? How do we love as John says? See 1 John 3:17–18; compare James 2:14–17 and Matthew 25:31–46.

57. Does Christian love happen automatically or do we have to work at it? Discuss the role of the Holy Spirit in the day-to-day life of saving faith.

58. Jesus was (and is) a friend of "tax collectors and 'sinners'" (Matthew 11:19; Luke 7:34). How can Christians follow Christ's example of love and friendship today?

Practical love within the family of God looks like God's love for us in Christ Jesus. If we love God, we love His children. That is, we value them, put their needs on a par with our own, and seek to serve them. (See Jesus' mission statement in Mark 10:35–45; compare Peter's recommissioning in John 21:15–19.) Jesus takes up His cross and walks to Golgotha to give His life as payment for our salvation. He does this in obedience to the Father, who sent Him for this very purpose. (Read John 10:11–18, especially vv. 17–18.)

The Christian, following in the Master's footsteps, denies the self and its needs and its agenda every single day. The believer, imitating the Master, daily takes up the cross of self-sacrifice and self-denial to serve fellow Christians and witness to the world (as Jesus says in Luke 9:22–23).

59. In Paul's list of virtues he places love first (Galatians 5:22). What can you now say about this fruit of the Spirit in light of Scripture's use of "love" between people? Summarize what you have learned.

Love is attitude. We love when we consider others of at least equal value to ourselves, worthy of our help, consideration, and kindness.

Love is action. Love moves us to act, to provide for the needs of others.

Love is emotion. Christian love involves the whole person—mind, will, body, and heart. We don't keep back part of ourselves when we love others as God has loved us in Christ Jesus.

Love is powerful. The Holy Spirit partners with us Christians in the day-to-day life we lead, as we follow in the footsteps of Jesus. (See 1 John 3:9 and compare with John 3:1–6; 1 John 4:7.)

Evaluating Your Love

The prophet David prayed, "Search me, O God, and know my heart; test me and know my anxious thoughts. See if there is any offensive way in me, and lead me in the way everlasting" (Psalm 139:23–24). Now that you have a clearer understanding of the love God calls you to in Christ Jesus, use the list below to grow in your understanding of this fruit in your life.

For each person or group on the list, consider (1) the love that person or group has shown to you, and (2) ways you have failed to share your love for that person or persons in Christ. Pray the prayer at the end of the list. Then draw up a plan to share God's love with those around you. For example, plan to say "I love you" to your spouse each day or give a thank-you card to a co-worker who has been a blessing to you.

The Lord   Family

Spouse   Congregation

Children   Pastor

Friends	Neighbors
Boss	Nation
Co-workers	Self

O Father of all mercy, You have begun Your work in me. Endow me more and more with all fullness of wisdom and knowledge. Then I may be assured in my heart and fully know how the Spirit, who has raised up our Lord, also enlivens the faith within me with the same power and strength. Through Him I have also risen from the dead by His mighty power, which works in me through Your holy Word.

Help me to grow in the knowledge of Your dear Son, our Lord Jesus Christ, and to remain firm in the confession of His blessed Word. Give me the love to be of one mind and to serve others in Christ. Then I will not be afraid of that which is disagreeable, nor of the rage of the "arsonist" (Satan) whose torch is almost extinguished.

Dear Father, guard me so that his craftiness may not take the place of my pure faith. Grant that my cross and sufferings may lead to a blessed and sure hope of the coming of my Savior Jesus Christ, for whom I wait daily. Amen.

(adapted from Martin Luther, 1483–1546)

Words to Remember

God is love. Whoever lives in love lives in God, and God in Him. 1 John 4:16b NIV

To prepare for "Joy Everlasting," read the Book of Esther.

3

Joy Everlasting

Happiness is a warm puppy.

Charles M. Schulz

Imagine Charlie Brown and Snoopy in a warm embrace and you've got the picture. Schulz also described happiness as "walking on the grass in your bare feet" and "the hiccups . . . after they've gone away." He provided wonderfully practical definitions of "happiness," giving us pictures that bring smiles to our faces and lift our spirits a bit.

But do these pictures help us understand what Paul means when he lists "joy" as the second "fruit of the Spirit" in Galatians 5:22? On the one hand, "joy" and "happiness" certainly seem to overlap. We can use both words to describe our feelings when we experience pleasure and respond to positive situations. In many ways, the two words are synonyms.

60. Write below three things that give you the greatest joy. We will return to this list at the end of this chapter.

The Joy of Rescue

According to the writers of the Old Testament, happiness may come and go but joy, anchored in God's love for us, endures forever. David writes about God's unfailing love as the basis for his joy in Psalm 21. As in other psalms, David places the key thought in the very center of the psalm (21:7) and echoes this theme in the first and last verses (21:1, 13). (He uses the same structure in Psalm 23.)

61. Read Psalm 21. What quality of God appears in both the first and last verses as a reason for rejoicing? What keynote does David sound in this psalm (v. 7)?

62. What "happy things" has God also granted to David (vv. 2–5, 8–12)?

As we saw in Psalm 21, believers rejoice in the strength and the unfailing love of God. These two attributes, or characteristics, of God come together when He acts to save His people from calamity or destruction.

Joy in Esther

The story of Esther describes how God delivers His people and their joy that follows. The setting for Esther is the mid-fifth century B.C. in the kingdom of Persia (modern Iran). God operates behind the scenes to save His people from an evil plot against them. Although the Book of Esther never specifically mentions God, the reader can plainly see Him at work through what appear to be coincidences and chance events.

63. Read Esther 3:1–6. Why does Haman hate Mordecai and the Jewish people so much?

64. What point does Mordecai make in 4:12–14 as he appeals to Esther for help?

65. What turning point occurs in the middle of the book (6:1–3)?

66. Why did the Jewish people celebrate Purim? How did they celebrate (8:15–17; 9:20–22)?

67. Would the Persian Jews have celebrated so joyfully if they had not learned about the earlier edict against them? Explain your answer.

The Joy of Salvation

The Feast of Purim illustrates the enduring joy of God's people, a joy we experience today through the feasts of Christmas and Easter. Though these events are long past, they bring enduring joy because God gave us salvation through them.

68. Many people find holidays depressing and lonely. Others wear themselves out with preparations. How does the story of Esther and the biblical teaching about holidays offer comfort and encouragement?

David had been the "apple of [God's] eye" (see Psalm 17:8; 1 Samuel 13:14). By trusting in the Lord he defeated Goliath (1 Samuel 17, especially v. 45). He refused to fight Saul, his father-in-law and king, even though Saul tried to kill David several times. He faithfully served the Lord for many years, and God promised that he would be the ancestor of the Messiah (2 Samuel 7:12–14).

Yet David also committed adultery with Bathsheba and murdered her husband and several other faithful servants of the LORD (2 Samuel 11). When the prophet Nathan confronted David, he repented of his sin

33

and wrote psalms expressing his repentance and faith (Psalms 32 and 51). Read Psalm 51.

69. To what quality or characteristic of God does David appeal for forgiveness (vv. 1–2)?

70. How can David say that he has sinned only against God when he has done so much harm to so many others (vv. 3–4)?

71. How deep does sin run in the human race (v. 5)?

72. What is the "joy of Your salvation," and how does one receive it (vv. 7–12)?

73. What model for the joyful life of the child of God does David offer us (vv. 15–19)?

Future Joy

Joy also looks forward. That is to say, the people of God experience joy in their lives regardless of the present circumstance because they look forward to the time when they will be directly in the presence of the Lord (Psalm 16; Isaiah 61; 65:17–25). Read Isaiah 12 and discuss the following:

74. To what "day" does Isaiah refer in 12:1?

75. Why does Isaiah rejoice when he considers that day? What has God done that inspires Isaiah so much?

76. When does that "day" dawn?

Joy in Service

Because Christ will return to grant you the fullness of His salvation, you can face each new day in joy. Like a child who joyfully counts down the days to Christmas, we joyfully count each day as one step closer to the fullness of our salvation in Christ. Come, Lord Jesus! Amen.

We do not live in a vacuum, nor do we experience joy as a purely abstract concept. God created us to work, serving Him throughout our lives (see Genesis 2:15). God warns His people about failing to serve Him gladly and willingly (Deuteronomy 28:47), yet the experiences of our lives often make it difficult to serve the Lord joyfully. How often we struggle to find the joy in our service when the responsibilities pile up and complaints come in! Read Ecclesiastes 11–12 and answer the following:

77. How does the author describe life in Ecclesiastes 11:1–6?

78. Read Ecclesiastes 11:7–10. What are the advantages and the dangers of youth?

79. Read Ecclesiastes 12:1–8. What are the burdens and disadvantages of age?

80. According to Ecclesiastes 12:9–14, what is the key to meaning in life?

Practical joy flows from a painful realization of our sinfulness and a clear appreciation for our salvation (1 Timothy 1:15). Add these to the list you made on pp. 29–30. Then plan to start each day with thanksgiving for the mercies of God (referring to your list, if necessary). This leads to a joyful attitude. As we will see more clearly in the New Testament, joy looks forward with great expectation and eagerness to the glorious arrival of the Messiah, while remaining firmly anchored in the Lord's gracious work and clear promises in the past.

Words to Remember

Restore to me the joy of Your salvation and grant me a willing spirit, to sustain me. Psalm 51:12

To prepare for "Joy Brings Endurance," read Philippians.

4

Joy Brings Endurance

May the God of hope fill you with all joy and peace as you trust in Him,
so that you may overflow with hope by the power of the Holy Spirit.

The apostle Paul, *Romans 15:13*

As we saw in the Book of Esther, the people rejoiced because God delivered them from death. Had they not known about the legal edict condemning them, their response would have been much different. Lasting joy, the kind of joy reflected in the New Testament, understands and appreciates our peril under God's Law and therefore rejoices in God's grace.

Joy Understands Sin

Paul tells us to rejoice in the Lord always (Philippians 4:4). We misunderstand him if we think that he directs us to put on a "happy face" and pretend everything's okay. His joy grows out of an honest and intense understating of sin and the sinner's condemnation by God's Law.

81. Read Philippians 3:1–11. In Paul's battle with legalizing Christians, he lists his credentials under the Mosaic Law for a self-made, right standing with God. What are his credentials?

82. What does Paul think of those credentials now that he is a Christian? Why?

83. How could Paul have such a positive attitude in the face of all his sufferings? (See 2 Corinthians 11:23–33 for a partial list of his sufferings, a fulfillment of Jesus' prediction in Acts 9:16.)

Joy Looks to Jesus

When the women went to the tomb on Easter morning, they expected to find a corpse. Instead, the angels told them that Jesus had risen from the dead and sent them back to tell this Good News to the other disciples. Matthew reports that they left the tomb afraid, "yet filled with joy" (Matthew 28:8). Real joy always looks to the crucified and risen Jesus.

84. Read John 16:17–24. Why were the disciples confused and upset?

85. Jesus plans to leave them for a little while and then return. What is He talking about?

86. What experience will inspire and complete their joy?

87. What does Jesus mean by "My joy" (John 15:11; 17:13)?

Joy Flows from Faith

Joy echoes throughout Paul's Letter to the Philippians like the bass drum in a musical performance. It sets the tempo and provides the theme of the Letter, especially in chapters 3 and 4.

88. Read Philippians 4:4–13. How can we genuinely and honestly "rejoice in the Lord always"?

89. What does the second coming of Christ have to do with our joy?

90. How do we avoid worry?

91. What is Paul's secret to contentment in any and every circumstance?

Christ the Ideal

The author of Hebrews wrote to Christians who faced serious persecution. They were tempted to give up Christ and return to Judaism, a protected faith in the Roman Empire. The author directed his readers to Christ as the pattern we should follow when faced with persecution and hardship.

92. Read Hebrews 12:1–12. What enabled Jesus to face the cross?

93. Because God has made us His own children through Holy Baptism, how may we regard suffering?

We can sometimes see a big difference between happiness and joy when we compare them in Scripture and note the points of contrast:

Happiness lasts for a time, but joy goes on indefinitely.

Happiness depends on circumstances, but joy exists apart from how things are going in our lives.

Happiness comes from inside us, but joy comes from God.

Evaluating Your Joy

The prophet David prayed, "Search me, O God, and know my heart; test me and know my anxious thoughts. See if there is any offensive way in me, and lead me in the way everlasting" (Psalm 139:23–24). Now that you have a clearer understanding of the joy God gives you in Christ Jesus, use the list below to grow in your understanding of this fruit in your life.

For each person or group on the list, consider (1) the joy that person or group has brought to you, and (2) ways you have failed to share your joy with that person or group in Christ. Pray the prayer and sing the hymn at the end of the list. Then draw up a plan to share God's joy with those around you. For example, plan a family outing just for the fun of it. Begin and end the outing with prayers of thanks to God for each member of your family.

The Lord	Friends
Spouse	Boss
Children	Co-workers
Family	Neighbors
Congregation	Nation
Pastor	Self

I thank You, my Creator and Lord, that You have given me these joys in Your creation, this ecstasy over the works of Your hands. I have made known the glory of Your works to men as far as my finite spirit was able to comprehend Your infinity. If I have said anything wholly unworthy of You, or have aspired after my own glory, graciously forgive me. Amen.
(Johann Kepler, 1571–1630)

Sing "Soul, Adorn Yourself with Gladness" (*TLH* 305; *LW* 239).

Words to Remember

Until now you have not asked for anything in My name. Ask and you will receive, and your joy will be complete. John 16:24

To prepare for "Peace amid Conflicts," read Ezekiel 34.

5

Peace amid Conflicts

We the peoples of the United Nations [have] determined . . . to practice tolerance and live together in peace with one another as good neighbors and to unite our strength to maintain international peace and security.

Charter of the United Nations, Preamble

On October 24, 1945, the United Nations officially came into existence. Delegates from 50 countries had worked for two months to write its charter in order to create an organization that would advance the cause of peace in a world torn by war. The nature of mankind, however, cannot be changed by charters and organizations. Conflict reigns supreme, reflected in such ordinary events as rivalry between siblings and strife between parents and children. This weakness of human nature has created one war after another, both large and small. The world lives in an everlasting state of war, relieved only occasionally by periods (often brief) of peace.

We might think of *peace* as merely the absence of war, and biblical writers often use the word this way. On the other hand, Scripture sometimes uses *peace* in a much different way. Rather than defining *peace* in a negative way (the absence of war), biblical authors sometimes think of *peace* in a positive, holistic way. Paul uses the word in this way in Galatians 5:22, when he includes peace as one of the "fruit of the Spirit" in the Christian life. In doing so, he stands on a solid foundation developed in the Old Testament and clarified in the New.

A Declaration of War

When God created the world, He created it to live in harmony. He designed human beings to rule over the rest of creation as His representatives (Genesis 1:27–28).

94. Read Genesis 2:4–3:19. The author describes three sets of relationships. How do the events of 3:1–6 change them? How does this change the relationship between humanity and the rest of creation?

95. How does this change the relationship between husband and wife?

96. How does this change the relationship between God and His image, mankind?

Peace, harmony, and order once thrived in paradise. After Genesis 3:1–6, war and disorder reigned through sin. Read Genesis 4:1–16 to see how sin looks as it grows up. Note the contrast between Adam and Eve's reaction to God's question (3:8) with Cain's reaction (4:9). Sin has produced a new attitude. It only takes a few generations for both righteousness (in Enoch, third generation; v. 17) and sin (in Lamech, seventh generation; v. 18) to fully mature.

97. Contrast Lamech's attitude in 4:23–24 with Cain's response in 4:9. What has changed?

God's Covenant of Peace

In the Old Testament, people "cut" covenants with one another as a way of making peace through agreements or contracts. In our society we sign papers detailing our mutual obligations. In the ancient world, one or more animals were sacrificed to "seal the deal." God established covenants with people using the same method. (Read Genesis 15:9–18 to learn about God's covenant with Abraham concerning his descendents. Notice the foundation of faith established in 15:6.)

In Ezekiel 34 God warns the leaders of Israel (the "shepherds") that He will hold them accountable for the welfare of His people. He condemns them for their sinful failure to lead Israel and promises to provide them with new shepherds.

98. Read Ezekiel 34:23–24; 37:24–28. Who will shepherd God's people?

99. What blessings are included in God's "covenant of peace"? (Note 34:25–31.)

100. When do God's people receive all the blessings?

The God of Peace

The pattern of sin, sacrifice, and peace come together also in the time of the judges (between the times of Moses and David). In Judges 6 God calls Gideon to liberate His people from the Midianites. When Gideon sees the Angel of the Lord, he becomes aware of his own sinfulness and fears for his life (Judges 6:22; see also Exodus 20:19 and Deuteronomy 5:25). The Angel of the Lord comforts him with the statement "Peace to you!" (translated from the original text). The Angel's "Peace to you" is identical to Jesus' "Peace be with you" on Easter evening (John

20:19, 21), except that "you" in Judges 6:23 is singular (addressed to Gideon) while "you" in John 20:19, 21 is plural (addressed to all the disciples in the room). In response to the Angel's word of peace, Gideon builds an altar.

101. Read Judges 6:11–16. What command and promises does the Angel of the LORD give to Gideon?

102. Read Judges 6:17–24. What does Gideon name this altar? Why?

103. Read Judges 6:25–32. What result did the commands from the Angel of the LORD bring in Gideon's life? the lives of God's people?

Peace comes through forgiveness. To put it another way, if the key to joy is gratitude, the key to peace is forgiveness. Peace between God and mankind requires blood sacrifice, the payment of death under the Law (see Ezekiel 18:4, 20; Romans 6:23). The Old Testament people sacrificed animals on the altars they built (see Exodus 20:24–26 for specifications).

104. To what greater event and blessing did the old covenant sacrifices point? Read Hebrews 9:24–26 and Romans 4:25–5:1.

The people had turned away from the Lord and worshiped other gods in the days of Gideon. God rescued them from their enemies but He also led them to repentance through the ministry of Gideon (Judges 6–8). No peace is possible where sin reigns. We cannot have both sin and peace. False prophets often proclaimed "peace" while ignoring idolatry and immorality, assuring God's people that they had peace with God at the very time when God was ready to go to war against them for their sin.

105. In Jeremiah 6 God warns His people and brings His charge against the false prophets. According to Jeremiah 6:16–20, why is the Lord angry with His people?

106. Read Jeremiah 6:13–15. What have the false prophets and corrupt priests failed to do? What have they done instead?

107. How does this apply to preachers and church leaders today?

As we prepare to turn to the New Testament, read Isaiah 9:1–7. In the middle of a long section on the Law, God shines the bright light of the Gospel about the coming Messiah. If God is the God of peace, the coming Servant will be called the Prince of Peace!

108. List the blessings that God promises through the Messiah in Isaiah 9:1–7.

109. How do these promises and blessings give you confidence in your service to the Lord and His people today?

Words to Remember

The LORD bless you and keep you; the LORD make His face shine upon you and be gracious to you; the LORD turn His face toward you and give you peace. Numbers 6:24–26

To prepare for "Peace without End," read Revelation 12.

6

Peace without End

The enemy is more to be feared and to be guarded against when he creeps on us secretly; when, deceiving by the appearance of peace, he steals forward by hidden approaches, whence also he has received the name of the Serpent.

Cyprian of Carthage (d. 258), *On the Unity of the Church*

Peace is such a great, yet elusive blessing. People will try anything from medication to meditation in order to experience peace. But peace is much more than something we experience. It is a gift from God, a gift the church can enjoy now and for all eternity.

110. Name some things people turn to in their quest for peace. Who is behind man-made promises of peace?

The Beginning of Peace

Luke records a powerful story about sin, forgiveness, and peace in his Gospel.

111. Read John 1:24–25 and Luke 7:36–39. Why do you think Simon the Pharisee invited Jesus to dinner?

112. What unusual things did the unnamed woman do?

113. Read Luke 7:40–50. What does Jesus mean by the last words He speaks in this story (v. 50)? How has He fulfilled the promise of these words?

Go in Peace

Not only do God's people go into the world at peace with God, at peace with people, and at peace within themselves, but they also face death in peace. In Luke's Gospel we read of an old man, Simeon, whom the Spirit led to the temple at the time of Jesus' presentation (as God had instructed Moses, Exodus 13:12–13). The Holy Spirit had told Simeon that he would not die until he had seen the Lord's Messiah.

114. Read Luke 2:21–35. Simeon's song is traditionally called the Nunc Dimittis (Latin for "Now dismiss," v. 29). Have you sung these words before? Where and how?

115. What does Simeon mean by "dismiss"?

116. How are "peace" and "salvation" connected for Simeon?

Peace in Christ Jesus

In Ephesians 2 Paul contrasts "then" (before the cross) and "now" (after the cross). In 2:1–10 Paul reveals the change Jesus effected in the relationship between God and humanity through the cross. In 2:11–22 he applies this to the relationship between Jews (who had God's Law) and the Gentiles (who were "outsiders" to God's covenant of peace in the Old Testament).

117. What is the "dividing wall of hostility" that separates Jew and Gentile (2:14)?

118. How did Jesus abolish that wall and bring peace to people?

119. By what means did the Ephesians receive this reconciliation? How has this blessing come to you?

The God of Peace and the Peace of God

Several times Paul describes God as the "God of peace" (Romans 15:33; 16:20; Philippians 4:9; 1 Thessalonians 5:23; see also 1 Corinthians 14:33). The author of Hebrews uses this same phrase and connects it to the blood of Jesus (i.e., His sacrificial death that seals the covenant).

120. Read Romans 5:1; 15:33; and 16:20 along with God's words to Eve and Adam in Genesis 3:15. What connects these passages? When does the conflict described in these passages finally come to a conclusion?

121. In symbolic language, Revelation 12 describes the spiritual conflict that lies behind the conflicts of this life. Read 12:1–9. Who are the combatants?

122. Read 12:10–12. How do the victors "overcome"? Does their victory guarantee physical security?

123. What are the implications of this for you personally? (Note also v. 17.)

124. Where does real peace come from and how does it spread in the world? (See 2 Corinthians 5:18–21.)

Beyond Understanding

The word *gentleness* in Philippians 4:5 refers to an attitude that does not insist on one's rights or welfare but yields to the needs of another. It can be translated "considerate," "thoughtful," or even "kind."

125. How does Philippians 4:5 reflect the "peace of God" possessed by a Christian?

Consider the spiritual and physical struggles of life and human attempts to understand and resolve such conflicts. In Philippians 4:7 Paul writes about the "peace of God," that is, the peace that comes from God through Jesus Christ.

126. Why does this peace transcend or surpass "all understanding"?

127. Worry robs us of peace. How does Paul's advice in Philippians 4:8 help us live in this peace?

Christ the Ideal

Read Philippians 2:1–11. Afflicted by false teachers (see 3:17–21) and torn by conflict (4:2–3), the congregation at Philippi seemed to lack peace. In 2:6–11 Paul holds high the picture of Christ at peace in His mission—the ideal we should imitate. Disregarding His own welfare and safety, Jesus gave up the joys of heaven to become a human being. He did not always use His divine power; He humbly resolved to bear the cross, dying the death of a slave and a criminal.

128. In this passage Paul does not encourage us to have a poor self-image. He asks us to think of others before we act or speak. In this study you have carefully considered the first three "fruit of the Spirit." How do joy and love come together with peace in Paul's counsel? See Philippians 2:2.

Evaluating Your Peace

The prophet David prayed, "Search me, O God, and know my heart; test me and know my anxious thoughts. See if there is any offensive way in me, and lead me in the way everlasting" (Psalm 139:23–24). Now that you have a clearer understanding of the peace God gives you in Christ Jesus, use the following chart to grow in your understanding of this fruit in your life.

53

For each person or group on the list, consider (1) the peace that person or group has shared with you, and (2) ways you have failed to live in peace with that person or group. Pray the prayer at the end of the list. Then draw up a plan to share God's peace with those around you. For example, if you have been at odds with a member of your congregation, go to that person and express your desire for peace. Pray for one another in Christ.

The Lord	Friends
Spouse	Boss
Children	Co-workers
Family	Neighbors
Congregation	Nation
Pastor	Self

Rule me, O God the Son, who has redeemed and ransomed me from sin. Take away from me the burden of sin committed during the week now past, and graciously grant me Your peace. You are the Supreme Bishop and Archshepherd of my soul. Help all servants of Your Word in this and all Your congregations on earth to labor and bring forth much fruit unto eternal life. Amen.

(Adapted from Johann Habermann, 1516–90)

Words to Remember

Peace I leave with you; My peace I give you. I do not give to you as the world gives. Do not let your hearts be troubled and do not be afraid. John 14:27

Leader Guide

This guide is provided as a "safety net," a place to turn for help in answering questions and for enriching discussion. It will not answer every question raised in your class. Please read it, along with the questions, before class. Consult it in class only after exploring the Bible references and discussing what they teach. Please note the different abilities of your class members. Some will easily find the Bible passages listed in this study; others will struggle. To make participation easier, team up members of the class. For example, if a question asks you to look up several passages, assign one passage to one group, the second to another, and so on. Divide the work! Let participants present the answers they discover.

Some excellent hymns that may be sung at the opening of each session are "Almighty God, Your Word Is Cast" (*TLH* 49; *LW* 342), "Salvation unto Us Has Come" (*TLH* 377; *LW* 355), and "The Fruit of the Spirit" (*AGPS* 225).

1

The Way of Love

Objectives

By the power of the Holy Spirit working through God's Word, participants will

- become more familiar with the way biblical writers use the word *love;*
- understand what God's command to "love your neighbor as yourself" (Leviticus 19:18; Matthew 22:39) entails;
- explain the distinctive fruit "love";
- identify specific ways to show God's love in their family, congregation, and community.

Begin with prayer. Read together the opening paragraphs and use the opening exercise.

1. Allow a few minutes for this exercise. You may allow some people to share what they have written but don't encourage group discussion yet. Let people answer for themselves.

Isaac and Rebekah

2. The firstborn son could expect to inherit the property of the parents. Often, the other children did not receive an inheritance. God told Moses that the firstborn son may inherit a double portion of his parents' property (Deuteronomy 21:15–17). Although Moses lived several centuries after the events of Genesis 25, the same practice was current in Isaac's day.

3. Favoritism is always a potential issue within families. The cultural rights of the firstborn, which God allowed, became a cause for jealousy. Our families still face the same issues today even though we live in

a very different culture. What parents haven't heard complaints about fairness from their children?

4. Answers will vary. Fairness is not only an issue for young children but also for adults. Who carries the burden of care for older parents? How will the inheritance be fairly divided after a funeral? Love differs from favoritism in that it is self-sacrificing.

5. Esau speaks sharply to his brother. He commands Jacob as if Jacob was an inferior person. Jacob's response seems like teasing. The rivalry and differences between the boys continues.

6. Isaac comfortably makes requests of his son and expects his son's obedience and attention. This demonstrates the trust and respect in their relationship.

7. Rebekah hatches a plot to steal Esau's birthright for Jacob. Jacob goes along with her deception. Rebekah does not fear that Jacob will betray her deception. Jacob clearly trusts his mother.

8. Rebekah plots against the plans of her own husband. She would deceive him! Apparently, she is not confident enough to speak with him directly about who will receive his blessing. However, she may be confident that he will forgive her deception in time.

9. Isaac doubts his son's words and puts him through a series of tests. Notice how sin has all but destroyed the family love of Isaac, Rebekah, Esau, and Jacob. Striving for one's own gain, selfish ambition, lying, and deception appear throughout this story. They also find a place on Paul's list of vices (Galatians 5:19–21). The leader of this session might also take the time to read Genesis 3 with the students to see how sin similarly affected our first parents.

10. First, Jacob gains the right and blessing of being the firstborn. He is now superior to his brother in the family (vv. 29, 37). Naturally, Esau feels betrayed by Isaac. He hatches his own plot to get revenge and regain his birthright.

11. God chose Jacob to be the bearer of the covenant promise. This doesn't mean that God predestined Esau to go to hell (an error taught by theologian John Calvin and others). It means that God chose Jacob to be the ancestor of the Messiah rather than Esau. The calamities described by Malachi (1:3–5) came upon Esau's descendants (Edom) because of their unbelief and their opposition to the descendants of Jacob (Israel).

God's blessings came upon Israel not because of their obedience or goodness, but because of God's loving-kindness and His promises to Abraham, Isaac, and Jacob. Through Christ, the Father extends His love, forgiveness, and blessing to all people, including the descendants of Esau.

12. We often think of love as an emotion, and it is. But biblical writers also use the word *love* in other ways. The use of "love" and "hate" in this passage refers to God's choice, an election by God in His plan of salvation. It does not teach a "double predestination."

Boaz and Ruth

The story of Ruth should do two things for the student: (1) teach the reader that love involves sacrifice and (2) introduce the concept of a kinsman-redeemer.

13. Ruth sacrifices her future in order to stay with Naomi. She gives up her people, her home, her culture, and even her national god for the sake of her mother-in-law. From Ruth's perspective (ably described by Naomi in Ruth 1:11–13), only poverty, hardship, famine, and an early death among strangers awaits her. This sets the stage for the surprising actions of Boaz, kinsman-redeemer for Naomi's family property.

14. Boaz first notices Ruth's youthfulness (v. 5). The foreman notes Ruth's kinship to Boaz through Naomi and describes her as a steady worker (vv. 6–7). Boaz describes his actions as a response to Ruth's love and care for Naomi.

15. Boaz purchases Elimelech's land and takes financial responsibility for Naomi and Ruth. The child(ren) from his marriage to Ruth would inherit the property rather than Boaz or his other children. Boaz's financial sacrifice is substantial, demonstrating his love for his broader family as well as his love for Ruth and Naomi.

16. The descendants of Boaz and Ruth include King David and "the son of David," Jesus. Jesus, our Redeemer, loved us to the extent that He gave His life as a sacrifice for our sins.

Erotic Love

17. God designed human beings for sexual intercourse. He blessed this aspect of His created order by calling it "good" (Genesis 1:27–28, 31). Through erotic love, the family comes into being. God describes this as a chief reason for marriage (Genesis 1:28; 2:24–25). Modern ideas about sex have undermined these important truths above love and marriage. For many people sex has become a recreation rather than the means of procreation and marital unity. How ironic that modern, industrial nations—the nations best prepared financially to bear and raise chil-

dren—are the nations experiencing depopulation! For example, the United States' population would be declining if it were not for immigration.

18. Point out that the terms by which the bridegroom addresses the bride reflect the marvelous diversity and complexity of marital love.

The bridegroom calls his bride his "neighbor" (2:2, 10, 13; 4:1, 7; 5:2; 6:4). The NIV renders "my neighbor" as "my darling," and a few other translations offer "my love" (KJV, NKVJ, RSV). The bride is companion to the bridegroom, as we see modeled in Genesis 2. Therefore, the point is made that "love your neighbor as yourself" begins at home!

19. The groom addresses his bride as his "sister" (4:9, 10, 12; 5:1, 2). He always uses another term to qualify "sister" so the reader does not misunderstand (usually "bride" but in 5:2, "neighbor" or "darling"). Of course, *endogamy* (the practice of marrying within one's family of origin) was common in the ancient world. For example, Abraham and Sarah were half-brother and sister (Genesis 20:12). Such unions were later forbidden under Mosaic Law (Leviticus 18:11). "Sister" in the Song of Solomon does not mean a blood relationship but reflects the family bond, the close and committed relationship created by marriage (Genesis 2:23).

In these passages the term that appears most often with "sister" is "bride." The Hebrew word can refer to a daughter-in-law, but it also can refer to a young bride, either just before or after the wedding.

20. Bring together these three types of love at this point: friendship ("companion," "neighbor"), family love ("sister"), and erotic love ("bride").

21. The author of the Song of Solomon describes the passion and strength of love in a series of comparisons: Love is like the mark of ownership provided by a seal. It is like a grave; it does not give up the one it receives. It burns like an intense fire, which cannot be quenched, like the "flame of the LORD."

22. Answers will vary.

23. A list may include the following: promises that fear and shame will be removed, the Lord is your Redeemer, He will call you back with deep compassion, everlasting kindness, and compassion.

24. Answers will vary. Emphasize the jealous love God has for His people (Exodus 20:5).

Friendship

25. Jonathan was King Saul's son and heir to his throne. Jonathan was old enough to fight alongside his father and to lead troops. According to 1 Samuel 18:20–21 David married Saul's daughter, Michal. This would make David a brother-in-law to Jonathan.

26. Distinguish a parity covenant (an agreement between equals) from a suzerainty covenant (a king's proclamation to his subjects). A list of covenants and brief definitions may be found in the *Concordia Self-Study Bible,* page 18.

27. David and Jonathan establish a parity covenant where they bind themselves in friendship by oath and offer mutual protection and welfare.

28. Answers will vary. Note the growth of the friendship between David and Jonathan. Also note the utter deterioration of David's relationship with his father-in-law (Saul). Friendships are important but rarely reach the level of importance and responsibility held by family members.

Did David keep his covenant with Jonathan (1 Samuel 20:16–17)? Read 2 Samuel 9 for the account of Mephibosheth, Jonathan's son, and "the rest of the story" (as Paul Harvey might put it).

29. Answers will vary. The priority of family usually outweighs every other relationship. However, there may be valid exceptions. Our first loyalty must always be to the Lord and His purposes. Read Matthew 12:46–50 for an example of this struggle from Jesus' life.

Love for God

We will delay our discussion of God's love for us until we reach the New Testament section, even though His gracious love appears throughout both testaments of Scripture. This session introduces the student to mankind's love for God. Here are several points to bring out:

Mankind's love for God involves all parts of a human being. The comprehensive "heart, soul, and strength" (or "heart, soul, mind, and strength" as Jesus renders it in Mark 12:30–31 and Luke 10:27) describes the extent and depth of our devotion and commitment to God as He requires it from us.

30. Genesis 3:1–7: Adam and Eve are asked if they trust God. They do not, choosing instead to trust themselves. It appears that since Eve does not immediately die from eating the fruit (see Genesis 2:17 for God's warning), Adam is willing to take a bite. He had been willing to let Eve act as the "test subject," and then joins her in outright rebellion and distrust.

Deuteronomy 6:1–3: God calls Israel to obedience. Using the form of a conditional covenant, God commands His people to obey Him (see again p. 18 of the *Concordia Self-Study Bible*). For a longer example of curses and blessings related to a conditional covenant, see Deuteronomy 27:14–28:68 (be forewarned—some of the curses are very graphic).

Jeremiah 2:2: God files a "breach of contract" complaint against Israel for covenant violation (see also 2:9; 25:31). Early in the "legal brief" (legal terminology appears at various points in Jeremiah's proclamations), God uses the language of a marriage contract to plead His case against Judah (2:2). That language reflects the passionate love that the bride and bridegroom displayed in the Song of Songs, now lost and forgotten.

Genesis 22:1–12: This illustrates the sacrificial nature of love. Verse 8 points ahead to the sacrifice of Jesus on the cross for our sins.

31. God commands us to love one another. This has little to do with affection and everything to do with attitude and values. God does not dictate that we have warm and fuzzy feelings towards one another. Rather, He commands us to put our neighbor's welfare ahead of our own or at least on the save level of importance. In other passages Paul describes love as the fulfillment of the Law. It is perhaps the one fruit of the Spirit that sums up all the others.

32. Answers will vary. A helpful definition for biblical teaching about love is this: love is wanting and doing what is best for another person. This is exactly how God has loved us in Christ. Since He wanted the best for us, He sent Jesus to take away our sins. He also bestows on us His Holy Spirit so that we may live by faith in Christ and bear much fruit.

2

God Is Love

Objectives

By the power of the Holy Spirit working through God's Word, participants will
- understand that God is the origin and source of genuine love;
- see how God's love transforms all human relationships;
- confess that Christ crucified provides the only hope of salvation and also offers the ideal picture of love: self-sacrificial, intentional, and unbounded;
- identify specific ways to love others with the love of Jesus Christ.

33. Answers will vary. An excellent example of this struggle is the desire to love someone in Christ struggling against carnal attraction or personality conflict. Many Christians want to forgive but cannot bring themselves to do so.

Family Love

God created mankind in His image and likeness (Genesis 1:26–27). Not only did He create individual human beings (Adam and Eve), but He also created the family (Genesis 2). In its structure and relationships, the family might be said to resemble the structure and relationships of the Godhead.

Paul works with this analogy in 1 Corinthians 11:2–16 as he directs the Corinthian Christians on the subject of prayer and prophecy in their meetings. The session leader could highlight the relationship between Father and Son, especially as portrayed by John in his Gospel and first Epistle. "Headship" and "submission" do not speak to the issues of a person's value or worth. Rather, they reflect the organization and structure of the plurality within a unity. Restored to a right relationship with God through Jesus Christ, the Christian also discovers what it means to be restored to a right relationship with other believers—family, friends, and spouse.

34. In John's first Epistle, he establishes the basis for the family bond that Christians have with God: the Gospel (defined as the Person, work, and the message of Jesus, taken as a whole). Note also the connection between the Gospel and the Holy Spirit. John makes this clear in his Gospel (John 3:34; 6:63; 14:26; 15:26; 16:13). The Holy Spirit unites Christians into one family through the Gospel, especially the new birth of Baptism (as Paul affirms in 1 Corinthians 12:13 and Ephesians 4:4–5).

35. In his first Epistle John uses the metaphor of light and darkness to describe the family characteristics of God's people and Satan's domain. For John (and for Jesus) no third option exists. Either one believes in Jesus Christ, enjoys fellowship with the Father, and lives in the light or one lives in the darkness, suffers the condemnation of the Father, and spends eternity with Satan. Love (self-sacrificial, all-encompassing, intentional) characterizes the family of God; hatred and murder (in the broad sense) mark the domain of Satan (Matthew 5:21–22). (See also John 1:4–9; 3:19–21; 11:9–10; 12:35–46; 1 John 2:8–10. Jesus identifies Himself as the "light of the world" in John 8:12 and 9:5.)

36. In John's writings, the "world" opposes God and rebels against Him. Even though He created the world and everything in it, even His own people would not receive Him when He came to them in the world (John 1:10–11). God's love, so different from human love in the fallen world, reaches out even to those who rebel against Him and reject Him. As Paul points out, God's love stands revealed at the precise point of the cross (Romans 5:8, 10). Jesus died for His enemies, that is, He died for the world (including us). The way God loved the world (John 3:16) should also be the way His children love the world. Recognize the difference between loving the world as God does (by the cross) and loving the world as fallen humanity does. A quick reading of Jesus' prayer in John 17 (especially vv. 13–19) might be helpful at this point.

37. This question raises the subject of sanctification (in the narrow sense of *practicing* our faith). God created a new person when we were baptized. That new person, spiritually alive through the gift of faith, works by the power of the Holy Spirit on a daily basis to produce good works (Ephesians 2:8–10). These are the "fruit of the Spirit" that Paul describes.

Righteousness may be defined as "covenant faithfulness," that is, doing what God tells us we should do in the context of a saving faith in His Anointed One (Ezekiel 18:5–9).

38. God defines His love for us at the cross. He then tells us that we should reflect this in our lives as well.

39. Love naturally spills over into other relationships from God, to us, to others. Genuine love cannot be isolated (that would be selfishness).

40. Draw a comparison to forgiveness. Now that we have been forgiven, we are obligated to forgive others (as in the Lord's Prayer, Matthew 6:12; 14–15; Luke 11:4; see also Matthew 18:21–35). As in the Sermon on the Mount (Matthew 5–7), the standard by which we live is the same standard by which God works with people. Because the old sinful nature still plagues Christians, sanctification (in the narrow sense) is a very rocky road. (See the Formula of Concord, Article II.)

Erotic Love

This section seeks to lead the student to a new appreciation for the structure in marriage (the husband as the head of the wife, the wife as helpmeet to the husband). Faith in Christ does not dissolve this structure, but it does radically change the way in which husband and wife function within it. The same could be said for all social relationships (as in Ephesians 6:1–9).

41. In the original language, no main verb appears in Ephesians 5:22. Most translations borrow the verb *submit* from 5:21, the hinge verse for this section. Paul uses the verb *obey* when addressing children (6:1) and slaves (6:5) and may well have that in mind in 5:22 as well. The common direction is about submission or obedience. This naturally sounds bad to modern ears since we live in an age of equality and political correctness.

42. Paul writes that husbands, parents, and masters are responsible for the good of those under their authority. They do not have authority to harm but to love, teach, and reward. He is also placing the wife, children, and workers *under someone's care*. To say "I don't need anyone else's care" is the same as saying "I don't need any loving relationships." This may begin as self-assertion but it ends as self-absorption.

43. The idea of being under another person's authority is repulsive to many today. We need to see in Paul's words more than a reference to authority. Christian love completely revolutionizes the marriage relationship. The structure of marriage does not provide the husband with a li-

cense for tyranny or abuse. Rather, it challenges him with a cross-shaped job description (i.e., a relationship of sacrifice). God's plan for husbands is that they sacrifice themselves for their wives, putting the welfare and needs of the wife ahead of their own (just as Christ did). Note especially 5:25b, where Paul explicitly reminds husbands that "love" is cross-shaped.

44. Paul uses the marriage relationship as a means for describing salvation. The intimacy and care in marriage most closely describes our relationship with Christ, our Savior.

45. "Mystery" refers to something that stands hidden behind something else; it cannot be seen and would never be discovered unless it was revealed. The "mystery" of marriage consists in its comparison with the Godhead (the relationship between the Father and the Son, 1 Corinthians 11:3) in two ways: headship and submission on the one hand and a plurality that becomes a unity on the other hand.

46. Perfect love drives out fear.

Friendship

47. Talk about the hostility between the Samaritans and Jews (going back to the fifth century B.C.). Jesus chose such bitter enemies to intensify His point in this story.

48. Jesus sets the boundary for love in answer to the question "who is my neighbor?" (i.e., "what are the limits for loving my neighbor as myself").

49. Jesus essentially answers that there is no limit to neighborly love. Christian love—self-sacrificial, expensive, unconditional, and intentional—must be offered to everyone with whom we come into contact, even (especially) our enemies. Jesus answers the rich young man with the Law (Matthew 19:16–24); He uses the Law to strip away the young man's self-justification. Christian love (reflecting and resembling God's love) does not ask for reimbursement. It takes risks, gives unconditionally, and meets the needs of others.

50. The short answer to this question is "we can't." In a sense, that is the point Jesus wants to make. We cannot fulfill the Law and earn salvation. It must come to us as a free gift of grace through the death and resurrection of Jesus. Yet the story of the Good Samaritan reminds us of the extent of our calling to "love our neighbor as ourselves."

51. Note the many characteristics of love. None of us lives up to this remarkable description except the Lord Himself.

52. All other gifts pass away. We will not need them in heaven. Yet love will remain. When Jesus returns in glory to judge the living and the dead, faith and hope will be replaced with present reality (as Paul points out in Romans 8:22–25).

53. Herein lies the daily challenge to every Christian. We don't bridge the gap in our behavior. Our love and good works come from the Lord! By the power of the Holy Spirit, we undertake each day to follow Jesus as His disciples and ambassadors of love.

Christ the Ideal

In this final section we see in Christ crucified our Savior and our role model. As leader, you may want to talk about Christ as God's "beloved Son," accenting the element of choice in that description. Comparing Matthew 17:5 and Mark 9:7 with Luke 9:35, we find that Luke uses "chosen" instead of "beloved" in the Father's description of Jesus ("beloved" appears in the KJV and NKJV). The idea of election as part of God's love for us has already surfaced ("Jacob I loved, but Esau I hated" [Romans 9:13; Malachi 1:2–3]). Move students to an understanding of Christian love as something intentional, a sanctified and personal choice.

54. Cain's act stems from selfishness. Christ's act stems from self-sacrifice.

55. The simple answer is no. Although Romeo and Juliet are portrayed as caring deeply for each other, their suicide reveals fear and insecurity. Suicide is different from self-sacrifice. Suicide is a selfish act, intended to end one's pain or even to harm the feelings of others. Self-sacrifice is always an act of giving, rescuing the life of another. The story of Romeo and Juliet brilliantly illustrates the power of passion. But it does not illustrate the power of genuine, godly love. One character tries to emulate God's love, yet stumbles in his efforts. Friar Laurence wants to save the lives of Romeo and Juliet and unite their families. (Consider reading the play or renting the movie and focusing on Friar Laurence's efforts.)

56. As a sinner, you are no doubt failing to love as you should. God may call us to be martyrs. But "lay down our lives" means more than dying for someone. It means lives of sacrifice, giving to meet the needs of others. It means not only speaking words of love and care, which are so needful, but also acting in love.

57. Christian love does happen automatically, but we also have to work at it. Both are true. The Holy Spirit works in us to will and to do

what is best. At the same time, the old sinful nature fights against the Spirit every step of the way. We cannot do perfectly what God commands, nor can we love others as God loves us in Christ Jesus. This is, however, our calling: to love as we have been loved, to give others as God has given to us, and to forgive as we have been forgiven. Finally, we do not trust in our work, even as Christians, to save us. We trust in Jesus alone. We do not rely on our own strength or understanding to live the Gospel in our daily walk with Jesus. Rather, we rely on the Holy Spirit as He continues to come to us through His Word and the Sacraments. Daily we take up our cross (self-denial, self-sacrifice, selfless love) and follow Him who died and rose for the world and for us.

58. God calls us to love even those who are difficult to love (e.g., the unfaithful, rowdies, the openly sinful, and socially unacceptable people).

59. Answers will vary. A good summary definition of a biblical view of love is this: Love is wanting and doing what is best for another person.

Encourage participants to put what they have learned into action by completing the closing exercise. Also encourage them to read the Table of Duties in Luther's Small Catechism as they consider how they will express their love in Christ through deeds. When they read about the duties "To Everyone," encourage them to think and pray about evangelism.

3

Joy Everlasting

Objectives

By the power of the Holy Spirit working through God's Word, participants will

- distinguish joy from happiness;
- understand joy as a gift from God;
- see that joy is a Spirit-worked attitude formed through faith in Jesus Christ;
- identify specific causes for rejoicing with family, friends, and others.

60. Answers will vary. Allow participants to share responses but don't enter into a group discussion or work toward a group definition.

The Joy of Rescue

61. The king and, by extension, the people stand secure in their joy through the unfailing love of God. David sets this at the center of the psalm, establishing this message as the keynote. The unity of the king and the people can be seen in the first and last verses, where David pictures first one and then the other as praising God. Both the king and the people rejoice in the Lord because of His unfailing love (*hesed*). This Hebrew term appears about 200 times in the Old Testament and occurs in God's explanation of the First Commandment in Exodus 20:6 and Deuteronomy 5:10 (part of the "Close of the Commandments" in Luther's Small Catechism); see also Exodus 34:7. God's unfailing love and His covenant faithfulness are bound very closely together (e.g., Psalm 106:45).

62. The people of God—king and subjects together—find security in God's strength. God's omnipotence comforts them (and us) because of His covenant faithfulness—His unfailing love. Note these two points:

- God's people rejoice in His power because no one can over-power God. (Asaph makes this same point in his appeal to God for help in Psalm 74. He also uses the same structure that David uses in Psalms 21 and 23, setting forth the theme of his appeal in the central verse, 74:12.) See also John 10:27–30.
- God's people trust in His unfailing love because He has prom-ised salvation to them and will not change His mind.

David's joy in the Lord's strength and salvation includes a heartfelt thanksgiving for other blessings as well: physical health, long life, royal power, victory over his enemies, and the destruction of his foes. God's favor involves both body and soul, faith and life. Along with spiritual blessings, the Lord grants material gifts. This "holistic" viewpoint is common in Scripture but must not be twisted into a "health and wealth" gospel. The believer does not trust God because God pays him off (Satan's accusation in Job 1–2). Yet Scripture affirms that every good gift comes from God (James 1:17; see also Deuteronomy 26:11).

Joy in Esther

The Book of Esther offers the student an opportunity to connect the joy of God's people with His gracious rescue from impending death. The degree of joy experienced by the Jews in Esther is directly proportional to the degree of fear they experienced when they heard about the legal edict declaring open season on them. In a similar way, the better we understand sin, the Law of God, and our predicament on Judgment Day, the greater will be our joy at the salvation we have received freely through Jesus Christ.

63. Haman was apparently an Amalekite. The Amalekites were de-scendants of Esau, the brother of Jacob. They had a "family feud" with the Israelites (Exodus 17:8–16; Deuteronomy 25:17–19; 1 Samuel 15; and 1 Chronicles 4:43). He plots to destroy the Jews in the Persian king-dom. Mordecai offends Haman's pride by refusing to bow down and honor him (Esther 3:1–2). This fanned Haman's hatred into full flame and sets in motion the events recorded in the Book of Esther.

64. He asks her to consider whether her high position might be more than personal good fortune. She may enjoy her status in order to serve a greater purpose (i.e., God has called her to rescue her people).

65. With the eyes of faith, the reader can see God at work throughout the story. The Lord of history works through seemingly unimportant details so that at just the right time things turn out the way He wants. Readers can see this especially in 6:1–3, where insomnia and a random choice of reading material set the stage for God's rescue of His people.

66. The Feast of Purim (from the singular *pur,* or "lot," from the casting of lots in 3:7) celebrates God's rescue of His people under Queen Esther. They observed the feast on the 14th and 15th of the month of Adar. They feasted, exchanged presents, and gave gifts to the poor. Sounds like Christmas!

67. As evident in 8:15–17 and 9:20–22, the people's joy flows from God's gracious rescue and the complete defeat of those who plotted against them (similar to Psalm 21). In a similar way, without knowledge of the condemnation of the Law we would not appreciate the blessing of the Gospel (see Galatians 3:24).

The Joy of Salvation

68. Answers will vary. The point of holidays (holy days) is to rejoice in what God has done for us and for our salvation. It is not in what we make of the holidays. The joy is there because the blessing of salvation is there. Lord, help us focus on that blessing!

69. David calls upon the unfailing love of God and His compassion as the grounds for an appeal to God for rescue.

70. The Holy Spirit has brought David to a fresh awareness that every sin against another person (particularly God's people) ultimately counts as a sin against God (cf. Matthew 25:31–46). Any assault or insult against another human being, created in God's image, attacks the Creator Himself (Genesis 9:6). Moreover, violence against a member of God's family is an attack on the head of the family.

71. David's confession of sin does not stop with his active disobedience to God. He looks back to the time he was born and even to the time he was conceived, confessing to God that he (and all of humanity) was God's enemy from conception (Romans 8:7).

72. By David's confession, he reveals the extent of sin in the human race. As we will see later, a deep sorrow over sin and a grasp of its extent and depth are fundamental to the "joy of Your salvation." (This psalm has served as resource for many Christian liturgies and hymns.) Joy overflows in the hearts of people saved from death.

73. David serves as a model for the life of a believer when he talks about a broken and a contrite heart rather than formal things like sacrifice

70

and offerings delighting the Lord. From this confession of sin and God's forgiveness flows the joyful life of righteous sacrifices and burnt offerings, pleasing to God through a childlike faith and trust in Him. The believer joyfully offers these costly gifts, not out of compulsion but out of gratitude. (See also Romans 12 for Paul's treatment of the Christian life as a living sacrifice flowing "logically" from justification.)

Future Joy

74. "In that day," writes Isaiah, referring to the Day of the Lord. It will be a day of judgment and condemnation for the unbeliever (Zephaniah 1:14–2:4) and deliverance for the people of God, both Jew and Gentile.

75. God has accomplished the salvation of His people through His Messiah and this inspires Isaiah to talk about the "glorious things" the Lord has done. Isaiah echoes the Song of Moses (Exodus 15:2), in celebrating God's gift of salvation through the Suffering Servant who would bear the sins of the world on the cross (Isaiah 52:13–53:12).

76. The Day of the Lord has already dawned in the person and ministry of Jesus Christ. Yet it must be said that the Day of the Lord has not fully risen above the horizon. Like Old Testament believers, the New Testament people of God look forward to the consummation of the ages at the coming of the Messiah.

Joy in Service

77. The author of Ecclesiastes looks at life from a human perspective. In 1:2 he pronounces it "pointless" (also translated as "vanity," "vapor," "meaningless"). His favorite phrase comes from a Hebrew word that ordinarily means "breath" or "vapor." It describes something that is very transitory, temporary, and insignificant. In Genesis 4, it is the Hebrew name of Adam and Eve's second son, "Abel," who lived such a short life. In 11:1–6 the author outlines how to live this short life to the fullest.

78. Young people enjoy the vitality and energy of youth. This, of course, has always led to trouble. How many older people don't regret the "sins of their youth"?

79. Old age brings with it a dulling of the senses, the loss of teeth ("grinders" in 12:3) and hair, the decrease of strength and vitality, and the multiplication of aches and pains. The author challenges young and

old alike to remember that the things of this world are passing away and that we all eventually stand in judgment before our Creator.

80. The key to a joyful (and meaningful) life, he suggests, is really very simple: trust God and do what He says. The writer tells us in 12:13b: "Fear God and keep His commandments, for this is the whole duty of man." To "fear God" includes the sinner's fear of punishment and the creature's respect and reverence for its Creator. However, the heart of the phrase "fear of God" is about saving faith, a trust in God that relies on His mercy and grace in time of need. From this saving faith flows obedience—the whole duty of mankind.

Since the lesson has raised the issues of past sins and present weaknesses, turn to Psalm 103:8–22. Read these verses responsively and rejoice in the Lord's full forgiveness for all of your sins through Christ Jesus.

4

Joy Brings Endurance

Objectives

By the power of the Holy Spirit working through God's Word, participants will
- acknowledge the completeness of our sinfulness;
- look to Christ for forgiveness and for joy;
- share the joy of new life in Christ with others.

Joy Understands Sin

When we think about the future, two things should shape our attitude: the cross and the final judgment. Confident of our salvation through the death and resurrection of Jesus Christ, we eagerly await His glorious return on the Last Day to judge the living and the dead (Romans 8:18–25). Christian joy does not depend on present circumstances or anything else in this world. It relies exclusively on Christ Jesus, on what He accomplished in the past and has promised to do in the future. The world cannot understand this.

Direct the participants to Philippians 3:1–6 to demonstrate this deep appreciation of the sinner's plight before God in St. Paul. Acquaint the students with the conflict in the early church over how much of the Mosaic Law should be required of Gentile converts (Book of Galatians). The Jerusalem Council resolved the issue in A.D. 49 (Acts 15) in favor of Paul's teaching, summarized in Romans 3:21–31.

81. In Philippians 3:1–6, Paul points out that from his earlier position as a rabbi and a Pharisee, he kept the Law without fault. Based on his own compliance with God's Law, he was confident of God's eternal approval. That confidence changed on the road to Damascus (see Acts 9;

22; and 26 for an account of his encounter with Jesus and his conversion).

82. Paul now realizes that all his credentials (listed in Philippians 3:5–6) are not just worthless, but are trash and even worse. The degree of Paul's emotion can be seen in the word translated by the NIV as *rubbish* (v. 8). In Greek this is the common word for human excrement! Isaiah used similar strong language in Isaiah 64:6. Paul wants to hit the reader hard with the contrast between the utter and complete condemnation of a sinner by the Law and the wonderful, amazing grace of salvation in Christ Jesus alone. The better we understand the Law and our condemnation under it, the greater will be our joy, regardless of the events of our lives.

83. Paul should have been miserable, depressed, and discouraged (2 Corinthians 11:23–33). Instead, he rejoiced, celebrating salvation from eternal condemnation, which was his punishment under the Law (Ephesians 2:1–4). Paul finds cause for rejoicing especially in his sufferings for the Gospel, for that is the cross-shaped, sacrificial life of Christ's disciple. In short, when the world mistreats us, abuses us, reviles us, persecutes us, and kills us—then we can have confidence that we've got the Gospel right, as Jesus predicted in Matthew 5:11–12; 24:9; Luke 21:12; John 15:20.

Joy Looks to Jesus

John 13–17 takes place on Maundy Thursday. Read through these chapters in preparation for this lesson.

84. The disciples followed Jesus because they believed Him to be the Christ, and they were right. However, they looked for an earthly kingdom of glory, and in this matter they were wrong. They expected Jesus to declare Himself publicly as Messiah at this Passover and usher in the glorious kingdom they awaited. Instead, He spoke of leaving them. This created a great deal of confusion and perhaps even anger among them.

85. Jesus challenges His followers to trust Him and speaks openly about the cross. He will leave them for a little while (crucifixion and death) and then return (resurrection).

86. Their grief will turn to joy when they meet the living, resurrected Christ.

87. Talk about joy as a gift from God when discussing "My joy" (John 15:11; 17:13). Jesus has two things in view (1) the joy that Jesus

has in communion with the Father and the Spirit; and (2) the joy He has as a result of accomplishing the plan of salvation. These form the foundation for the joy experienced by Christians. Believers rejoice in the fellowship we have with the triune God (1 John 1:1–7). Remind the students of the joy of John the Baptist at the presence of Jesus (Luke 1:44), the joy of the Magi at seeing Jesus (Matthew 2:10), and the "good news of great joy" brought by the angels at Jesus' birth (Luke 2:10).

Joy Flows from Faith

88. Paul bases his admonition to rejoice on the Lord's promise to return. Because Jesus died and rose for us, His return publicly vindicates the Gospel and ushers in the new heavens and the new earth. The kingdom of glory is coming! Therefore, we can rejoice at all times, regardless of how things are going in our lives or in our world.

89. We know the outcome because we know that Jesus will come again to judge the living and the dead and to raise all believers to eternal life.

90. The "gentleness" of 4:5 refers to the quality of yielding our own wants, desires, agenda, and goals to others. We don't insist on our own way and we don't "look out for number one." We practice consideration, looking to the welfare of others rather than ourselves (as Jesus did perfectly; see also Philippians 2:1–11). Part of the "art" of living joyfully includes a focus on others rather than on oneself.

91. In 4:12 Paul uses a word that frequently described initiation into the mystery cults of the day. He writes "I have learned the secret," or perhaps better, "I have been initiated into the secret" of knowing how to be content regardless of circumstance. He spells out the "secret" in 4:13, "I can do [am enabled in] everything through Him [Jesus] who gives me strength." Paul does not say that we can reach any goal we choose if we only have faith in Christ. What he says is that he can face anything and everything that comes his way because Jesus strengthens and empowers him through faith. Paul does not espouse a "theology of glory" in 4:13 but expresses his confidence that nothing can separate him from the love of God that is in Christ Jesus our Lord (Romans 8:28–39). That faith serves as the fountainhead for the joy that flows into this Letter and into his life.

Christ the Ideal

92. On the other side of the cross stood the glorious throne of God. Once Jesus accomplished the plan of salvation, He resumed His position at the "right hand of the throne of God" (a Near Eastern expression describing the official who runs the kingdom). God justifies us through the death and resurrection of Jesus Christ (the cross). That alone rescues us from God's wrath on Judgment Day. The cross also provides the working model for discipleship, especially for living the joyful life in Christ.

93. The author of Hebrews asks us to understand our troubles, especially persecution, as a reflection of the cross of Christ. Suffering and hardship aren't signs that God has forgotten us. Just the opposite is true! They are proofs of God's love for us, just as the cross stands as the ultimate proof of God's love for you.

5

Peace amid Conflicts

Objectives

By the power of the Holy Spirit working through God's Word, participants will
- recognize that a state of war exists between God and humanity because of sin;
- realize that peace (holistic, positive) must come as a gift from God;
- rejoice in the reconciliation that Christ has accomplished at the cross;
- experience the personal peace that passes all understanding.

Open the study by introducing the subject of war and peace. The history of the United Nations (and the League of Nations before it) illustrates mankind's futile attempts to impose peace upon society. We live in a natural state of war, and periods of peace are few and far between. Help the students consider the origin and nature of the hostilities into which we are born in order to appreciate God's solution at the cross.

A Declaration of War

94. By rebelling against God (Genesis 3:1–6), Adam and Eve created a permanent state of war. God created mankind to manage creation, ruling it as His representatives. As a result of sin, creation would rebel against humanity (Genesis 3:17–19).

95. The war between the sexes had begun! The "desire" of the wife in 3:16b refers most likely to the "desire to control" (as also sin "desires" to control Cain in 4:7).

96. The ultimate consequence of mankind's war against God is death, as God warned in 2:17. Yet Eve did not die when she ate the fruit of the tree of the knowledge of good and evil (a fact not lost on Adam, who was with her). Perhaps Adam thought the serpent was right when it promised that she would not die when she ate (3:4). She served as the "guinea pig" in the experiment and, seeing that she survived the fruit, Adam also ate. God may have passed over this particular sin (and many more afterwards), but He ultimately atoned for all sins in Christ crucified (as Paul points out in Romans 3:25–26).

97. You could compare Cain's reaction to God's question in 4:9 to that of a two-year-old in the midst of the "terrible twos" or a teenager in a rebellious phase of life. Adam and Eve had hid when they heard God coming. When questioned, they tried to shift the responsibility for their sin to someone or something else. Cain, on the other hand, challenged God.

Lamech, the seventh generation from Adam on Cain's side, showed the full maturity of sin. He boasted that he would kill a man for merely wounding him (disproportionate justice) and that he was at least 11 times more important than God (77-fold vengeance versus 7-fold vengeance). Pride and self-centeredness lie at the heart of the war between mankind and God. Contrast the approach of Jesus in Matthew 18:21–22 where the same 7-fold/77-fold formula appears! This provides a real key to understanding "peace" as a gift of the Spirit through forgiveness.

God's Covenant of Peace

Consider talking about the custom of "cutting a covenant" in the ancient world. Blood sacrifice sealed the covenant and bound the two parties together in the contract. Sometimes these covenants resembled modern contracts (*parity* covenants, i.e., covenants cut between equals) and sometimes they resembled declarations from our governmental leaders (*suzerainty* covenants, where no negotiations or bargaining took place at all; see the *Concordia Self-Study Bible,* p. 18 for more information on covenants). Critical to God's covenant of peace is the coming of the Messiah, David's son, and His sacrifice as the Good Shepherd (John 10). Note two important aspects of this covenant of peace: it is "cut" exclusively by the coming Messiah and it is holistic.

The Hebrew word *peace* includes material things as well as spiritual: rest from enemies, freedom from hunger, prosperity, and all other blessings of body and life. Peace comes to us exclusively through Jesus

Christ, "cut" at the cross. Peace is fully bestowed on His people after Judgment Day in the new heavens and the new earth. We have these now in Christ, but they are not yet fully bestowed.

98. Israel Himself, through a descendant of David. (We might remember 2 Samuel 7:8–16 as the place where God promised that the Good Shepherd, the Messiah, would be a descendant of David.) In the middle of God's comforting promise through Ezekiel, He tells His people that He will cut a "covenant of peace" with them.

99. The blessings include a land free of wild beasts, safety, blessing for Israel's neighbors, rain, fruitful trees and crops, security, rescue, and knowledge of the Lord's presence. These blessings correspond with the blessings and curses of the covenant given through Moses. (See Leviticus 26.)

100. This covenant is the new covenant promised through Jesus Christ. (See Jeremiah 31:31–34 and Hebrews 8:7–13.) It is the covenant of peace that you enjoy through the death and resurrection of Jesus for the forgiveness of your sins.

The God of Peace

Introduce the Old Testament figure called "the Angel of the LORD," from Exodus 3. Note that verses 2 and 14 provide strong evidence that the "Angel of the LORD" is God Himself, most likely the Second Person of the Trinity.

101. The Angel tells Gideon to go save Israel and promises to go with him and smite the Midianites.

102. He called it "The LORD is Peace" because the Lord promised peace to him.

103. The commands did not bring the peace we might expect. Gideon ends up in conflict with the people of the region and prepares for war with the Midianites.

104. There could be no peace with God without payment for sin. Jesus put an end to the old covenant sacrifices by completing what they could not do, by atoning for all sin and granting perfect peace with God.

105. The people refuse to listen to Him and reject His Law. Even though they offer excellent and exotic sacrifices, the Lord is not pleased.

106. By glossing over the sins of the people and promising "peace," the prophets and priests deceived the people of God and failed in their basic duty to warn the community and teach them the truth.

107. Modern Law-and-Gospel preaching seeks the same goal as the true prophets of old: warn unrepentant sinners of God's impending wrath so that, by the power of the Holy Spirit, people might repent and hear the sweet Gospel of peace through Christ Jesus—the ultimate sacrifice.

Draw attention to the promise of a coming Messiah (Anointed or Chosen One). Isaiah 9:1–7, especially verse 6, serves this purpose very well.

108. The blessings include an end to gloom, future honor, national growth, joy, deliverance from the oppressor, destruction of the bloody garments of war, a new government through a child ruler (Christ), and a never-ending kingdom and peace.

109. The Lord keeps His promises! Even though you may be experiencing turmoil, cling to God's peace, joy, and love given to you through Christ Jesus. Pray confidently for the rule and intervention of Jesus in your life. He will hear your cry and come with His blessings.

6

Peace without End

Objectives

By the power of the Holy Spirit working through God's Word, participants will
- confess that Christ gives us peace through His forgiveness;
- recognize that the peace of God does not mean we will never experience conflict in this world;
- share the message of reconciliation with those who don't know the peace of God.

110. Answers will vary. People have turned to various religions, financial security, charismatic leaders, self-righteousness, and even isolation. Satan stands behind every man-made "offer" of peace.

The Beginning of Peace

111. Just as the Pharisees had questioned John the Baptist's ministry as a prophet, so they also questioned the validity of Jesus' ministry. Verse 39 reveals Simon's thoughts about Jesus. We don't know for certain why Simon invited Jesus to dinner, although it happened more than once (see Luke 14:1–14). Perhaps it was due to Jesus' popularity or reputation. Whatever the reason, Simon showed great disrespect to Jesus by his lack of hospitality. This creates a tremendous contrast with the sinful woman's behavior. The type of sentence in 7:39 is called a "contrary to fact" sentence. That is, Luke constructs his sentence to signal to the reader that Simon does not think Jesus is a prophet, much less the Messiah. Simon is thinking, "If He were a prophet (which He is not), He would know who is touching Him and what kind of woman she is (which He does not)—a sinner."

112. She crosses several cultural lines—touching Jesus, unbinding her hair, entering the Pharisee's house uninvited, and washing and anointing Jesus' feet. Through her actions, her faith in Jesus shines as brightly as Simon's unbelief, revealed in his lack of hospitality.

113. Jesus tells several people "Your faith has saved you" in the Gospels: the woman with the chronic flow of blood (Matthew 9:22; Mark 5:34; Luke 8:48), the Samaritan leper (Luke 17:19), blind Bartimaeus (Mark 10:52; Luke 18:42), and the sinful woman (Luke 7:50). Does Jesus mean only that their faith has healed them from a particular disease, or does He mean that their faith has saved them from God's eternal wrath?

The Greek word for "saved" can refer to a rescue from disease (or other predicaments), but these stories contain several hints that Jesus means much more than "made well" when He says, "Your faith has saved you." For instance, in Luke 17:11–19 all 10 lepers are healed, but only the Samaritan leper hears the comforting words "Your faith has made you well [saved you]." Of the 10, only the Samaritan worships at Jesus' feet. The story in Luke 7:36–50 is even more helpful because the woman who is "saved" suffers from no physical disease at all. In fact, Jesus speaks of forgiveness immediately before He tells her, "Your faith has saved you," indicating that He means "saved from God's eternal wrath."

True peace is the consequence of faith, forgiveness, and rescue from God's righteous anger. God sends us into a world of hostility, danger, and war to live in peace—peace with Him through Christ Jesus, peace with others by His cross, and peace within ourselves as a gift of the Spirit.

Go in Peace

114. Class members should be familiar with Simeon's song as part of the Communion liturgy. The Mosaic Law required presentation (Exodus 13:12–13) and an offering for newborn children like Jesus.

115. Simeon says, "Now dismiss Your servant." Given the context (especially v. 26) "dismiss, send away" is a euphemism for "let die." It seems most likely that Simeon has in mind his own death when he offers this prayer.

116. Simeon's song directly connects "peace" and "salvation." Inspired by the Holy Spirit, Simeon recognized Jesus as the One who would bring both war and peace (see Luke 2:34–35). He speaks his

prayer as he holds the infant Jesus in his arms. The infant Jesus is the "Salvation" Simeon sees. We can also face death in peace.

Peace in Christ Jesus

117. The "dividing wall" that formerly separated them is the Law, as Paul makes clear in these verses.

118. Paul contrasts "before" and "after" pictures of God and people (Ephesians 2:1–10) as well as of Jew and Gentile (Ephesians 2:11–22). The cross marks the point at which everything changed. Paul goes so far as to speak of Jesus as "our peace" (2:14). Peace between God and mankind comes exclusively through the initiative and action of God. He resolves the problem of sin at the cross (remember that the key to peace is forgiveness). The state of war between humanity and its Creator ends with the sacrificial death of Jesus on Good Friday. The early church took several years to figure out how this affected the division between Jew and Gentile, as recorded in Acts 15. Approximately 10 years after the Jerusalem Council (note the decree in Acts 15:23–29), Paul writes to the Christians in Ephesus about the unity that Christ won for all believers, Jew and Gentile alike.

119. Baptized into Christ, Christians are "dead" to the Law and free from its rule and regulations (see Romans 6:1–4). This does not provide a license to sin, but it does eliminate the distinction between those who were part of God's covenant of peace (the Jews) and those who were outside of it (the Gentiles). The Holy Spirit unites all believers in Christ Jesus (see Galatians 3:26–29). This is made possible exclusively at the cross. God established peace with the world through Jesus' death (His "blood" of the covenant; see Matthew 26:28; Mark 14:24; Luke 22:20; 1 Corinthians 11:25), and that peace came to the Ephesians personally through the preaching of the Gospel and Baptism. Objective peace (with the world) becomes subjective (personal) through the means of grace (Word and Sacrament) because through these means we receive the forgiveness of our sins in Christ's blood.

The God of Peace and the Peace of God

This section introduces the "ministry of reconciliation" entrusted to the church by Jesus (Paul's terminology in 2 Corinthians 5:18). As Christians spread the Gospel, they bring peace to people mired in a spiritual war. Jesus calls believers "peacemakers" in Matthew 5:9 and refers to them as "sons of God," a Semitic way of saying that they share the qualities or characteristics of the God of peace.

120. Genesis 3:15 records the first Gospel promise of a Savior. New Testament authors never cite this passage, but it is easy for Christians to see a strong reference to the coming cross—apparent defeat followed by joyful victory over sin, Satan, and death. God reconciled the world to Himself at the cross, and Jesus commissions His church to spread that word of reconciliation and peace.

121. A woman (the people of God), a red dragon (Satan), a male child (Jesus), God, the archangel Michael and his angels.

122. They overcome Satan by the blood of Christ (the Lamb) and by the Word. Note that they still faced death. Their victory is spiritual security but not necessarily physical security.

123. We enjoy peace with God through the Gospel. However, Satan will not make peace. In fact, he rages all the more against the people of God.

124. Real peace comes from God alone, who reconciled us to Himself through Jesus and has made us "the righteousness of God." Through us God makes His appeal to the world, calling all people to reconciliation and peace.

Beyond Understanding

125. In Philippians 4:4–9 Paul gives some very practical advice concerning this peace. It passes all understanding (note that the original text does not have "human" in the sentence—this peace passes *all* understanding) because it depends on faith in Christ Jesus, not on circumstance or events in our lives. Paul makes the same point in Romans 5:1. We often forfeit our sense of peace when we focus on harmful or sinful things.

126. Peace with God changes our attitude. Instead of insisting on our own right (e.g., our place in line at the grocery store or our spot in heavy traffic on the highway), we practice our faith by yielding to the needs of others (Philippians 4:5). Ironically, putting into practice this attitude of Christ (see Philippians 2:5–11 in the next section) actually helps our sense of peace to flourish and grow. Also, we trust that our future, even this very moment, comes with God's foreknowledge and blessing. He is guiding our lives even in the midst of chaotic events.

127. We worry when we doubt God and look to our own resources, the circumstances that surround us, and the problems that face us. (Consider Matthew 14:22–36, where Peter takes his eyes off Jesus, sees the

wind and waves, and sinks. Jesus' words in Matthew 14:31 still "sting" today when we give up our peace for worry, doubt, and fear, only to realize at the end that we were in Jesus' hands all along.) Paul advises us in Philippians 4:8 to focus on healthy and uplifting things, an excellent tip for peace and tranquility. We often create a negative and destructive "internal dialogue," which poisons our attitude and actions. Paul directs our thoughts to those thoughts that are worthwhile and consistent with our faith in Christ.

Christ the Ideal

128. Much ink has been spilled on this passage over the years. Focus on the attitude displayed by Christ Jesus, especially at the cross. Peace with God moves us to yield our own rights and privileges for the sake of others, as did Jesus in His mission and ministry. We may well be the "wronged" party in a conflict, yet it is better to forgive as we have been forgiven than to "get even." Paul talks about his "joy" in 2:2. Perhaps a good analogy would be how parents feel when all the kids get along and love one another instead of fighting and arguing. Love motivated Jesus to the cross. It moves us to forgive as well.

Glossary

calling. See **vocation.**

covenant. A relationship or agreement not based on kinship. A contract. A "parity" covenant is an agreement between equals. A "suzerain" covenant is an agreement between a lord and his servant or between a strong nation and a weak nation.

double predestination. The false teaching that God eternally decreed who is to be saved and who is to be damned (with no hope of repentance).

election. From the Latin word "to choose." The biblical teaching that God chose believers through Christ to be His people and to inherit eternal life. God chose them purely by grace and not because of their good works or their faith.

fruit of the Spirit. Effects produced in believers by the indwelling of the Holy Spirit (Galatians 5:22–23). The good works produced by faith in Christ.

fear of the Lord. Reverence and trust in the Lord.

Gospel. The message of Christ's death and resurrection for the forgiveness of sins. The Holy Spirit works through the Gospel to create faith and convert people.

holistic. Applying to a whole subject. In theology, teaching that applies to a person as a whole instead of focusing solely on the spiritual or physical aspect of a person.

holy. Set apart for a divine purpose (e.g., Holy Scripture is set apart from all other types of writing). The Holy Spirit makes Christians holy (see **sanctification**).

justification. God declares sinners to be just, or righteous, for Christ's sake; that is, God has imputed or charged our sins to Christ, and He imputes or credits Christ's righteousness to us.

kinsman-redeemer. A person responsible for protecting vulnerable family members, especially in areas of inheritance.

Law. God's will that shows people how they should live (e.g., the Ten Commandments) and condemns their failure. The preaching of the Law is the cause of contrition.

parity. See **covenant.**

repentance. Sorrow for sin caused by the condemnation of the Law. Sometimes *repentance* is used in a broad way to describe all of conversion, including faith in God's mercy.

Sacrament. Literally, "something sacred." In the Lutheran church a sacrament is a sacred act that (1) was instituted by God, (2) has a visible element, and (3) offers the forgiveness of sins earned by Christ. The sacraments include Baptism, the Lord's Supper, and Absolution (if one counts the pastor as the visible element).

sanctification. The spiritual growth that follows justification by grace through faith in Christ.

Semitic. From the Hebrew name *Shem*, who was an ancestor of the Jewish people and other Near Eastern groups (Genesis 10:1, 21–31). A word used to distinguish the descendants of Shem and their culture (e.g., Hebrew is a *Semitic* language).

suzerain. See **covenant.**

theology of glory. The idea that the true knowledge of God comes from the study of nature, which reflects God's glory. Also, the belief that suffering should not be part of the Christian life because God's people always triumph.

vocation. From the Latin word for "calling." A person's occupation or duties before God. For example, a person may serve as a father, a husband, and an engineer. Each "calling" comes with different responsibilities.